YOU CALL, WE HAUL

The Life and Times of Bob Carter

D1388248

Mat Ireland

This book is dedicated to the Trans UK drivers who are no longer with us

You Call, We Haul

Old Pond Publishing is an imprint of Fox Chapel Publishers International Ltd.

Project Team
Vice President–Content: Christopher Reggio
Associate Publisher: Sarah Bloxham
Designer: John Hoch

ISBN 978-1-912158-40-9

A catalogue record for this book is available from the British Library

Fox Chapel Publishing
903 Square Street
Mount Joy, PA 17552, U.S.A.

Fox Chapel Publishers International Ltd.
7 Danefield Road, Selsey (Chichester)
West Sussex PO20 9DA, U.K.

www.oldpond.com

We are always looking for talented authors. To submit an idea, please send a brief inquiry to acquisitions@foxchapelpublishing.com.

Printed and bound in China

22 21 20 19   2 4 6 8 10 9 7 5 3 1

CONTENTS

Bob (far left) and former drivers after lunch at the café.

FOREWORD

I want to thank Mat and Simon personally for their unrelenting energy and enthusiasm on this whole project. I never envisioned when Mat arranged the reunion back in 2005 that this would have come about as a result; it was a magical evening to see the drivers again after all the years.

To me, those dozen or so who did the Middle East work for me cannot be praised highly enough. Without them, Trans UK would have been just another container haulier from Felixstowe. Mat is now the closest thing to one of my Middle East boys with his travels in a truck. If he had been a young man back then knocking on my door for a job, there is no doubt in my mind that I would have taken him on – sometimes you just get a sense or good feeling about someone, and that rings true about him.

Bob Carter
Ipswich, September 2016

I first heard of Mat Ireland in 1999. At the time he was working for Haven Logistics at Felixstowe as an import clerk. I was Karl 'Fluff' Freeman's night shunter, an owner driver who was pulling ro-ro trailers on behalf of Haven. His girlfriend at that time was Haven's traffic planner. Fluff suggested Mat and I would get on well together as we had a common interest in trucks. We wrote to each other, initially exchanging notes and photographs, before we actually met in person.

Mat had previously attended college with Lewis Rowlands, whose father Paul is a veteran of the overland runs to the Middle East. Paul went on to write his memoirs in a book called *Not All Sunshine and Sand*. Mat was a catalyst in this project. He has a fascination with long distance road haulage. It was through Lewis and Paul that Mat organized a reunion for ex-Trans UK Director Bob Carter and as many ex-employees as could be contacted. This occurred at The Douglas Bader pub on Martlesham Heath on Saturday, 19 November 2005. Mat encouraged me to attend the reunion. I had met Bob Carter once when he was in the Melton HQ of his brothers' firm, W. Carter Haulage. I knew Mervyn Woollard, having worked with him at Russell Davies, and I knew the names Fred Grimble, Keith Williams and Mick Coombes from contacts in the haulage industry. I was surprised Geoff White, who then worked for trailer operator Autocontex, was there. At the time it was my largest DGSA client. I had no idea Geoff used to work for Trans UK in the administration department. It was well attended, which shows the high regard Bob's ex-employees still hold for him. Keith Williams came over from Belgium especially.

Bob kindly paid for a buffet, which we all enjoyed. It was a great evening and Bob was visibly quite overwhelmed with the whole thing. So many people made an effort to come nearly twenty-five years since his companies had ceased trading! Mat created an opportunity to reunite so many old friends and gave others a further opportunity to make some new ones.

Bob asked me if I could create something on Trans UK in 2012. I had so many commitments that I simply did not have time. I had my own small fleet of trucks then, which never allowed me any free time for myself. Mat said he would 'have a go' but was a bit daunted by the project. I said I would help him in every way I could. It has been made harder by his job as, working with Transam Trucking doing concert tours, he is away for literally months at a time.

Being involved in the creation of this has been magical. Bob Carter alone is a living legend. He has become a good friend along with several other drivers. I've only met 'Smudger' Smith three times. Gerry Keating I have never met at all but, listening to their taped interviews, I do not feel a stranger.

It is sad that 'Taffy' John Dinwiddy died while driving a truck for Bob Carter and Micky Prigg, Mervyn Woollard and Fred Grimble have all passed away since the 2005 reunion.

Bob's photographs and passion for what he has achieved in his life are the core of what we have put together here – we could not write things down fast enough. He went from tea boy to running his own fleet of more than forty trucks, and then into the aftermath of Trans UK. In 2016 he still works part-time in the office of the fleet department for Argos, doing the deliveries to houses, aged 78. He wouldn't be beaten by anything. There is some irony in semi-retirement as he lives in the same bungalow he grew up in as a child, having seen a lot of the world in between and experienced much. I was aged just 10 when Trans UK ceased trading but I can still vividly recall Bob's Fiats and the grey, red, black and white livery. Being introduced to Bob's brother, 'Wardy', in 2015 was a special day. To have got close to some of the men that made this happen has been a privilege and an honour.

I am proud to call these men my friends and share in their achievements. This book needs to be created for a current generation to share and future generations to learn from. Going to Turkey in a Volvo F86? A touch of insanity required I think!

L–R: Lenny Balaam, Mick Prigg, 'Smudger' Smith, Mervyn Woollard, Mick Coombes, Paul Rowlands, Ray Rainham, Keith Williams, Fred Grimble. Seated: Brian Wales & Bob Carter.

Remember, modern day life cannot continue without trucks. Empty factories. Empty shops.

Simon Waspe
Ipswich, September 2016

Bob (centre) en route to Christmas Island.

BOB CARTER, THE EARLY YEARS

ROBERT LESLIE 'BOB' CARTER WAS BORN ON 2 JULY 1938 in Melton, Suffolk. One of five children, his Father Lesley owned a small local haulage company that operated out of The Cherry Tree pub in Bromeswell, a couple of miles down the road.

He was educated firstly at Melton village school, and then at a school in Ipswich. He didn't enjoy his time in education, preferring to be working with his hands on something mechanical.

The family haulage company at The Cherry Tree pub at Bromeswell, 1957.

"The best time for me was the school holidays, when I could hang around my dad's haulage yard," he recalled. "One favourite highlight for me would be when me and my brothers used to go with dad to Rush Green Motors for him to look at second-hand trucks. 'Tubby' Green, the owner, used to give us a pound note and tell us to, "Bring the old bugger back again!"

In 1953, at the age of 15, Bob left school and started working for the family company as a yard boy, making tea and running errands on his bike.

"It was like getting paid for what I used to do in the school holidays! Back in those days you didn't really think about what career path you were going to follow when you left school. For example, if your dad was a bricklayer, you could end up being a bricklayer, or a chef's son might follow his father's profession, that's just how it was. So it didn't even cross my mind about doing anything other than getting involved in the family company," says Bob.

A large amount of Carter's work involved tipper trucks working on the local RAF base at Bentwaters, and Bob would often go and spend the day up there driving a small tipper truck. As he was driving on private land, having no licence was not an issue.

This was the time when National Service was still compulsory, and Bob's sign-up date was looming. However, if you were involved in a job of national importance, i.e. agriculture or coal mining, you could apply for special dispensation to exempt you, something a number of the local farmers' children had claimed.

I was 17 and decided that as I enjoyed working on heavy vehicles the most suitable job for me would be in the REME

Bob decided that rather than be conscripted into a job in the Army that he didn't have any interest in, he would sign up early of his own accord, which would then enable him to choose his own career path.

"I was 17 and decided that as I enjoyed working on heavy vehicles the most suitable job for me would be in the REME (Royal Electrical and Mechanical Engineers)".

Having been accepted, Bob was sent to Blandford Forum in Dorset for his basic training, and on completion he was then temporarily posted to Taunton in Somerset, before being moved to Herford in Germany for his first proper posting in a Light Aid Detachment, or LAD: 118 Company RASC.

Depending on Army requirements, Bob's LAD was attached to various REME companies. It was tasked with things such as escorting convoys in case of breakdowns and covering general repairs.

Bob's attitude to life was slightly different to a lot of people in that many will tell you to "never volunteer for anything", but he was just the opposite.

"If there were courses coming up, I would always volunteer to go on them. For example, I completed a fuel injection course in Duisburg, followed by a heavy plant course back in Bordon, Hampshire, which enabled me to get back to England

Bob, back row, third from the right, after completion of a course at his posting at Taunton.

for a little while. My view was it would be useful to maximize my mechanical knowledge while someone else was paying for it!"

Back in Germany, after completing his courses, he was driving in the Harz mountains on an Army recovery job and thought he would give his sergeant a bit of a scare.

Driving a Scammell Pioneer recovery truck, more commonly known by anyone who drove one as a 'pot boiler', while towing two Austin K9 'wireless wagons', he decided to take it out of gear and get up a little bit more speed. Scammells generally had a top speed of around 28mph, although the drivers would often attach a piece of string on to the throttle that would take it up to about 35mph.

As the speed increased, Bob realized that he was struggling to get it back into gear and the vehicle was accelerating out of control! Luckily for Private Bob Carter, with his local knowledge of the roads he managed to steer it into an escape lane and bring the lot to a stop. His plan had worked, and the sergeant was scared witless, as was Bob!

Austin K5 loaded with bridging equipment on manoeuvres in Germany. They were nicknamed 'Austin screamers' due to the loud transmission whine they gave off when being driven.

Bob on a day off in the local town of Bad Salzuflen, near to his base at Herford, Germany.

The Army barracks at Herford.

Bob and his colleagues posing on a Scammell in Germany.

Bob with a Commer-cabbed Ford Thames V8 petrol engine truck on manoeuvres in the German forest.

A day out to the German grand prix at the Nürburgring, 1957.

An action shot Bob took of his colleague's Scammell.

Bob, in the centre, at Paddington station en route to Christmas Island. To his left is Ray Wilson, who became a close friend and work colleague.

The pits at Nürburgring.

The Qantas Super Constellation that Bob flew on as far as Hawaii. The plane suffered from several minor troubles, delaying their overall travel time by a few days.

Bob at Goose Bay, Labrador, Canada.

The main REME workshops, Christmas Island, which was to be Bob's new home for the next year.

Another view of the garage.

Ever cab happy, Bob at the wheel of a Scammell before taking it on a road test after repairs. The truck was coupled to a Tasker low-loader with 'four in line' axles at both ends of the trailer.

Bob seen here with a Bedford RL, taken inside the Royal Army Service Corps (RASC) depot.

Bob, third from left, with his new work colleagues. Taken outside 'C' section, which was where heavy vehicles and plant equipment were repaired.

Another view of the workshops. 'C' section is seen on the left-hand side.

The only person to work on any of the Euclids on the island, thanks to his previous training in Germany before his posting.

Christmas Day on Christmas Island in 1958. Bob posing with some coconuts, which servicemen used to post home to their families. They simply painted the address on them and the Army would fly them home and deliver them. The practice stopped in the end as there were simply too many and too much weight to handle.

After successfully repairing the gearbox on the Caterpillar D8, Bob is seen here giving it a test run. While repairing it, his colleagues removed the gearbox inspection plate and found a large adjustable spanner laying inside the gearbox! No doubt this did not help the vehicle's performance.

The Land Rover that Bob and his colleagues rebuilt using scrap parts. His sergeant was not very impressed by their actions!

Bob performing a repair on the hub of one of the Scammells.

Another shot before the Land Rover was repaired. For an island with no traffic other than the Army, accidents seemed quite frequent, and often quite damaging.

Using a Scammell to recover a stricken Albion tipper truck that has sunk into the soft ground of the island.

Another Land Rover that was repaired and put back into service.

Another recovery job, this time to free a bogged down AEC mobile crane. This is quite a rare colour photo.

Bob and two friends on leave in Hawaii.

While on leave on Hawaii, Bob would often take a tour around on a bus. Most of these were powered by two-stroke diesel engines, which would leave a ringing in the ears!

About a year into his posting, he was told, "Pack your gear, you're off home!" He was leaving Germany.

"I had one week's embarkation leave before having to report to Arborfield near Reading. After my dad had finished work for the day, he drove me back from our home in Suffolk.

"It was late in the evening when we arrived, and the soldier on gate duty was busy on the phone. I left my leave pass on his desk at his post, and he gave me a wave of acknowledgement in return."

The next day on parade, when everybody's names were called out for duty rosters, Bob's name wasn't mentioned, so rather than query it, he just made his way back to the NAAFI and sat drinking tea and relaxing for the rest of the day. Not only did this happen the following day, but the day after as well!

Bob knew what day he was meant to be leaving for his new posting on Christmas Island, so decided not to bother with the parade.

A friend of his then found him and told him that he had been reported AWOL!

"I couldn't believe it!" said Bob.

"The 'red caps' had been dispatched to my house, and my father was livid, telling them that he had taken me personally back to the base!

"I went down to the adjutant's office to find out what had happened. When we checked back at sentry post at the main gate, we found my leave card had slipped down the side of the desk. Fortunately this misdemeanour didn't go on to my record, as I wasn't actually AWOL. Surprisingly, they decided to send me back home for a few more days leave before once again reporting back to Arborfield.

"I was then sent back home for yet *another* week's embarkation leave before reporting back for the final time, flying out to Christmas Island in late February 1958. I had been getting a bit fed up with the going back and forth, but at least my mother, Isla, was pleased to have me home whenever the opportunity arose.

I had no idea what Christmas Island was or even where it was!

"At the time I had no idea what Christmas Island was or even where it was! And I think it was only because I had volunteered for so many different courses that I had been selected to go out there.

"We were flown out on a Qantas civilian flight, via Prestwick, Reykjavik, Newfoundland, Vancouver, San Francisco and Honolulu. It took us five days!

"This was, of course, the era before jet engines and our plane kept being delayed, mostly with radar problems. It was difficult to find one's way across vast ocean stretches by sight alone!"

For the final leg of the journey to his Christmas Island posting, Bob had to board a military plane. "It was the worst plane I have ever been on!" he complained.

"After crossing the world in a nice civilian plane, we boarded this former World War Two Hastings transport plane. There weren't any proper seats, just slatted benches down the fuselage sides. It was well past its sell-by date! There were rivets missing everywhere and the windows rattled in their frames! Good grief, 600 miles in this old bus. There was *no* food, so if you had forgotten to have your breakfast you starved, and the noise and draughts were just incredible!

"When we finally landed and disembarked the heat and humidity hit us straight away," said Bob. "It was like trying to breathe custard."

For a young lad from sleepy Suffolk this extreme heat was quite a shock.

"I was there as an LAD attachment to the Royal Army Service Corps. They were the truck drivers for the Army and as part of their remit were in the process of building the runways and road infrastructure on the island. As the 'attachment', we were there for the repair and maintenance of all their machinery, and it was a full-time job as the vehicles were properly 'abused' by the drivers!"

All these preparations were for the new H bomb tests that were scheduled to happen in the area, not that the recruits had any idea what they were there for when they arrived on the island. It was all very secretive.

During my time there, seven bombs were tested; four were land-based atom bombs, shot from barrage balloons.

"During my time there, seven bombs were tested; four were land-based atom bombs, shot from barrage balloons. The other three were H-bomb 'atmosphere tests', the ones everyone has seen on news reports over the years with the 'mushroom cloud'.

"The thing is, looking back, the protection we were offered was very amateurish. These were still very early days in nuclear testing, and other than the catastrophic damage a nuclear explosion could cause no one was really aware of the physical and internal harm radioactive fallout could do, too. None of us knew what was going on and we just followed orders.

"We were told to detach the sides from the tents we were living in, but to leave the roof on. All vehicle windows were wound down and Land Rover windscreens folded flat to the vehicle body.

"The whole testing programme was incredible and like nothing else I have endured in my life.

"We were told to get on our knees and bend forward, placing the heel of our hands into our eyes, with the backs of our hands pressed tightly to our knees in a sort of foetal position.

"Then, through gigantic megaphones, the countdown would begin, ten, nine, eight, seven, etc. down to one, followed by a deathly silence for a second or two until the sound and light waves hit you. It was like looking at an X-ray of your whole body, such was the brightness of the light, and the heat blast was like being

Looking out over Pearl Harbour on the flight back to Christmas Island.

Show me the way to go home! Bob posing with the various city destinations and mileages to them.

Bob with a Bedford RL, being used as transport for some of the troops to go swimming. Bob was always the designated driver for these trips, but he relished the chance of a stint behind the wheel.

Loaded with barrels of bitumen on the roll collected from the docks, the Scammell rests back at the service corps depot after a short but strenuous drive.

A Scammell and AEC parked in the barracks. Note the lack of windscreen in the AEC; if they broke engineers would not bother replacing them due to the heat of the island.

A line-up of petrol-engined Albion 10-tonne tippers, seen at the service corps.

Shortly before the Duke of Edinburgh was due to visit, it was decided that the workshops needed tidying up . . .

And everything was thrown in and buried! Note that a lot of the trucks are actually American that were left behind after the Second World War had ended.

And so a few large trenches were dug . . .

enclosed in a room packed full of three-bar electric fires.

"The blasts even knocked all of the coconuts out of the trees!" remembered Bob.

During the tests, the local people were taken off the islands by the Royal Navy and kept at sea for a couple of days before being returned, all this on the assumption that any pollution had been blown away!

You might think that some of the locals and staff based there must have been affected in the long-term by this testing, but funnily enough Bob was not aware of any deaths or adverse effects on anyone at the time or since and shows no signs whatsoever of any problems himself, although his family does have a history of living a very long time.

Bob and his new colleagues soon became accustomed to their new posting, working twelve hours a day, six days a week, on maintenance and repair work.

"It was quite surprising how many accidents people have when there's only palm trees and each other to hit!" he laughed.

Bob, as the sole qualified person, was the only fitter allowed to do any work on the huge Euclid Scrapers, something for which all the volunteering back in Germany was now paying dividends.

A lot of the repairs were of the 'mend and make do' variety and all older and wrecked vehicles were kept as donors for repairs that might be required, and there were many.

One such donor repair job Bob had was for a mobile crane that had broken down. Built by F. Taylors, the Taylor Jumbo was based on a Fordson

It was quite surprising how many accidents people have when there's only palm trees and each other to hit!

The remains of a Morris one-tonner, which was nicknamed the Morris pig, destined for the trenches to be buried out of sight.

Major tractor. This particular crane's differential had broken and was beyond repair, and so it was immobilized. After making enquiries about a replacement 'diff', Bob and the workshop were told it would take roughly six months for a new one to arrive with them via sea freight. This amount of time really was not an option, and so Bob set about the scrapheap looking for something suitable. Lo and behold, a one-tonne Morris truck axle was found that looked like it would fit with a little ingenuity. Sure enough, Bob and his colleagues managed to fit the replacement axle and get the crane moving again. But when it came to the test run, something was amiss. Instead of having four forward gears and one reverse, the crane now had four reverse and one forward! After a lot of head scratching, Bob came to the conclusion that the pinion was on the wrong side of the crown wheel to work as the broken one had done. Despite this, the regular driver was still happy to drive the crane, as it proved to be a better set-up for him to move around the island, he simply had to look over his shoulder to be going forwards.

> *On the quiet we had rebuilt an old Land Rover for use as 'private' transport for ourselves.*

All spares had to be either flown or shipped in from the UK, in fact virtually *everything* had to be flown in from the UK!

A useful find were the many old American army vehicles left behind after the Second World War. These were kept behind the workshops, and one day Bob and a couple of his young workmates, trying to combat the boredom, had an idea.

"Unbeknown to our sergeant, and although we shouldn't have," said Bob, "on the quiet we had rebuilt an old Land Rover for use as 'private' transport for ourselves. It had been deemed a write-off by our corporal and was being kept for spare parts.

"All was going well until we got too cocky and drove it across to the cookhouse, where it was spotted by our staff sergeant.

"Where'd that come from," he blared out, soon noticing it was one of the write-offs by its identification number. Although he was annoyed at them for rebuilding it, none of them was actually disciplined for disobeying orders. Instead, he made Bob park it in the middle of the parade yard and crush it with a D8 Bulldozer! After that it was well and truly written off!

Bob's childhood surrounded by the sounds and activities of transport business had left a deep impact on him.

"I was already very cab happy, and would jump at any opportunity to take trucks out for road tests when they came out of the workshop after repair."

Quite often one of the six-wheeled drive Scammell ballast trucks had to be driven to the port to load drums of bitumen for the road and runway gangs. They were loaded three across on the roll, chocked, and three high. It was about a

25-mile journey to the port and back, and this would take about half a day in all with the lack of roads and the loading procedure. Bob's hand was always the first in the air to volunteer for this run.

The Duke of Edinburgh was scheduled to visit the island in April 1959 and, as the place was a little unkempt, the soldiers had to tidy the whole base and make it more presentable. That meant all the 'scrap' donor vehicles, and any general old rubbish, had to be gone or hidden from view! Being a small island in the middle of the Pacific, this wasn't going to prove an easy task. It was decided that several large trenches were to be dug, and everything that was deemed as 'scrap' was to be put in the trenches and buried. It really was a waste of resources, but orders were orders. This was at a time when the environment and the impact of people's actions on it were not considered. Needless to say, the Duke's visit passed without a scare and he never passed remotely close to the 'scrap' trenches.

Now the locals still believed that the world was flat, and that if you walked far enough you could fall off its edge

"The locals on Christmas Island were ever so friendly to us. One man in particular used to regularly come and clean the REME's club bar for us, and early on we found he had a taste for beer. One particular occasion, from what we could gather, while he was busy cleaning up the bar area, he must have drank all the alcohol dregs from the previous night's binge, and for the first time in his life he was drunk.

"Now the locals still believed that the world was flat, and that if you walked far enough you could fall off its edge, so, as he was very drunk, to stop himself, he'd stabbed himself through his own hand into the wooden table! Needless to say, we didn't see him again after that episode."

Bob's posting was for just over a year, by which time he'd completed his regular enlistment and was due for demob. He had the option of either flying straight home, or to wait for a good friend's demob a week or so later. Being impatient to get home he decided to go straight away instead of hanging about. He flew back exactly the same route he had come, only to find out from his friend at a later date that he had returned via Singapore and Australia!

"If I hadn't been in such a hurry I would have had a complete round the world flight courtesy of Her Majesty!"

THE FAMILY BUSINESS

W HEN BOB GOT HOME FROM BEING DEMOBBED it was back to square one, as far as he was concerned.

"My father had a very dim view of Army fitters for some reason, and as we didn't see eye to eye from the get-go, I started right back at the bottom!"

Carter's Haulage was heavily involved with the local pea harvest each year, and Bob was put on to nights as a fitter in case anything went wrong. It was mostly issues such as punctures that needed addressing at night, anything major was left until daylight and the dayshift. The pea season lasted about two months. If someone didn't turn up for their night shift, Bob was put behind the wheel and they just went without a fitter for the night.

Following on from the pea season would be the bean season, and once again Bob was on nights but this time as a driver, collecting from the farms locally and delivering to Birds Eye's plant at Lowestoft.

Bob was getting tired of the lack of any organization within the yard and workshops, something he was not used to dealing with. "I tried to organize the stores as it was a nightmare! There wasn't any system or order, and I tried putting my Army experience to good use. I shelved the pub cellar out, and organized the whole lot for them. When my father saw it he went mad! I simply couldn't believe it! After that episode I pretty much gave up in the workshop and went driving instead."

This was about 1961. The majority of the work was to the London markets, again at night. The truck would be loaded in the yard and off Bob would go, normally in a four-wheeler Bedford, but sometimes in a different truck if the Bedford was not available.

> *I tried to organize the stores as it was a nightmare!*

Bob's second articulated lorry. Not many other people wanted to drive this truck due to its 'two stick' gearbox and bad brakes. It is seen here loaded with waste cardboard from Saxmundham for delivery to Purfleet for recycling.

One evening, Bob came in to find he had to drive the fleet's only articulated truck for the night. After already putting in a full day's work behind the wheel, he arrived back in the evening only to be told he had to go down to make several drops at the London night markets that night. His protests about the fact that he had already done a day's work fell on deaf ears. The three markets were Spitalfields, Borough and Covent Garden, with several drops in each market. "I was trying to get used to having to reverse the thing. This was the first 'proper' articulated vehicle I had driven, on Christmas Island the set-ups had been a lot different, and there was not really any reversing going on anyway. It took me so much longer than what it would have taken if I had been there with a rigid. By the time I was finally empty, all the trucks that were offloading were long gone, the buyers had all come in to buy their items for their shops, and it was daylight!"

He then had to go to Spillers Mill, Silvertown, east London, and collect a load of chicken feed to return to Nayland in Suffolk. By the time he got back to Marks Tey in Essex he was exhausted, but he knew that if he took the loaded trailer back his father would go mad. Instead he dropped the trailer at the farm and went home with just the tractor unit. "Needless to say my father went mad anyway, saying they needed the trailer for a night run that night back down to London. To be honest I was so tired I didn't really care and just went straight home and to bed!"

To be honest I was so tired I didn't really care and just went straight home and to bed!

In all his time working at Carters, Bob was never given a brand new truck. He was always handed one down that someone else didn't want. The Foden that Bob had as a regular truck was originally a four-wheeler rigid, which had been bought

An overview of the W. Carter haulage yard. The company had moved here from its previous site at The Cherry Tree pub at nearby Bromeswell in 1958. The site remains in the family today, and it still used as a transport-related yard.

One of the trailers of timber loaded from Felixstowe for onward delivery.

A health and safety officer's nightmare! Loading 'Heysham flats' with groupage in Carter's yard.

Loaded with 21 tonnes of dried pulp from the long gone sugar beet factory at Ipswich. The photos are taken at Turner's (Soham) storage facility at Martlesham aerodrome.

Parked in the yard ready for the off. Bob's AEC is on the right, both with unaccompanied ferry trailers.

Loading peas from Birds Eye's factory in Lowestoft. The Carter trucks would have delivered the peas from the field, and now the fridge trailer owned by Continental Ferry Trailers was being loaded for Italy. This would go to Felixstowe for unaccompanied shipping and onward delivery on the Continent.

Waiting to load sugar beet from a Suffolk farm. Carter's driver 'Fabulous' can be seen on top of his load.

With an unaccompanied French-owned trailer for onward delivery.

Waiting to load fertilizer at Cliff Quay, Ipswich. It was loaded directly from the boat and taken to Fersfield, near Diss in Norfolk.

Carter's trailers stood down at Felixstowe docks loaded with timber. All these would have been loaded by hand in various lengths straight from the ship, and were awaiting delivery.

A Saturday morning in the yard. The Commer on the left had recently been involved in an accident in Ipswich town with a double-decker bus. It is without its livestock body and awaiting repairs.

from Marston's Flour Millers at Icklingham in Suffolk. There was a family connection there as Bob's cousin was married to one of the Marston brothers. The Foden had been converted to an articulated tractor unit by Marston's own workshops. It had a 'twin stick' gearbox and vacuum brakes, which when it got going would fly along, but stopping it with the vacuum brakes was difficult, and took longer than other trucks on the road due to their inefficiency. This was most probably why no one else at the firm wanted to drive it. This was also the truck with which Bob had his biggest scare in his driving career.

While en route to Scotland on a Sunday loaded with potatoes, he was going across the A66 heading towards Penrith. Dropping down into the town of Appleby, they were having one of their annual fairs. Due to the lack of efficient braking, Bob was on the brakes harder and harder, yet they were having no real effect. He threw on the 'dead man's brake' (a trailer brake operated from within the truck), as well as the handbrake as far as that would go on, yet the truck wouldn't come to a stop. Somehow he managed to get through the town without hitting anything or anyone, and managed to come to a stop in a small garage on the other side of the town. When he got out, he could smell the paint from the front drums! An hour after stopping Bob was still shaking with adrenaline after the ordeal.

Bob was also unlucky enough to jackknife twice in one day while driving for Carters! Driving a Dodge artic with a 'four in line' trailer (these trailers had all of their four wheels across one axle at the rear of the trailer), Bob had delivered barley to the maltings in Felixstowe docks and was returning for the next load. He was coming down Brightwell Hill near Waldringfield. He had to press the brakes, and the whole truck and trailer was sent sideways across the road. Fortunately, it all went into the entrance of a local quarry, so Bob just pulled back on to the road and carried on. Only a couple of miles further along the road, near Martlesham, the same thing happened again! This time though the trailer was more or less pressing on the back of the cab, and the front of the unit was sent into the bank, so it was wedged in. The first truck to come across the scene was an eight-wheeler rigid behind him, who kindly put a chain on the back of the trailer and gave it a good pull, which managed to pull the whole lot back and round. The front bumper was slightly bent, and Bob was a little shaken and his pride a little dented but other than that everything was fine.

Due to Carter's rural location, a lot of their work came from agriculture as well as the forestry work that was going on in Suffolk. There would be trailers loaded with timber every day for the Celotex mill in Neasden, London, as well as the board mill at Sunbury-on-Thames. The mill at Sunbury had a restricted height access, due to the location of some of the mills pipes going across the entrance. Bob soon learnt that any trailer heading here couldn't be loaded up very high. "The first time I went down to Sunbury I couldn't get in, the load was too high! So I had to borrow a small cart, and unload the first few layers of logs just so I could get in to carry on unloading. After that I made sure to only load one log higher than the headboard of the trailer."

> *The first time I went down to Sunbury I couldn't get in, the load was too high!*

A lot of the London work would be back loaded from the American forces' stores in Surrey and Commercial docks in east London for their air bases around Suffolk. The drivers would always hope for a load for the base at Bentwaters so they could get home for the night. This was good paying work as they would sometimes pay for two full loads on one trailer due to the way it was organized. Heavier loads would pay by their weight, whereas anything light would be paid by its cube. So if they floored the trailer out with something heavy, they would often then load on top with something such as toilet rolls, which were light. This was classed as two different loads, despite the truck being within the law.

Bob was one of a group of six drivers who took the first ever deep sea containers from Felixstowe docks. Two of Carter's trucks were joined by two from D. R. Munson's of Hadleigh, and two from Ferrymasters. All bar one of the trucks had 33ft trailers, the exception being one of the Ferrymasters trucks, which had a stripped down tilt trailer, which was 40ft long. This meant the containers would overhang the trailers by 2ft, which was standard practice then. The boxes were for an American company called Sealand. The ship, the *Sealand Fairland*, had berthed in Felixstowe over the weekend, and the containers were loaded straight on to the trucks. All of them were loading from the Dumbarton bond in Scotland, with full loads of whisky for export to America. They were to load, and then meet the ship again at Grangemouth docks, as it was equipped to offload the containers itself. Bob set off on Sunday for Scotland. All the trucks were loaded on Tuesday morning, and customs sealed. They asked the security man at the bond if they could stay in the bond for the night due to the load and its security. They were told that they had nothing to worry about.

Loading the timber on to the conveyor. If you got on this side for delivery it was a sight quicker than having to unload it all and restack it, which had to be done to the left.

Bob's friend, Les. Originally from Jamaica, Les had come to the UK in the early immigration programme on the banana boats. A lot of his friends had gone to drive buses, but Les had found work at the wood yard. Hard working, but laid back, Bob got on well with him during his time delivering to the yard.

Showing the lack of headroom, Bob soon learnt not to load higher than the headboard of the trailer, otherwise you would end up unloading and reloading just to get into the factory to then unload yet again!

Unloading both on to the conveyor and also restacking ready for when the factory needed them, this is the 'slower' unloading bay.

A Guy Big J4, as yet unregistered but destined for the now defunct MAT Transport, takes part in the demonstration day.

Showing off the potential of the operating tipper. Note the Page brothers' Guy tractor unit in the background, a name that will appear again later in Bob's life.

A 'four in line' aggregate trailer on display. Four in line refers to the axle having four wheels in one line instead of on two axles. This enabled the loading of extra two tonnes per axle.

The Hoynor site in Essex.

Bonneted Mercedes showing off a new tipper trailer.

"Someone in the council houses outside would have been watching what you all loaded. They know its J&B whisky you have loaded, and as you can't buy that in the UK it's not worth ripping off as they can't shift it," they were told.

So off they all set for Grangemouth. On arrival there, the ship had been delayed, so they arranged for the trailers to be dropped in the customs yard at the docks for security, and they all set off for some digs in Falkirk. They ended up staying there for two nights waiting for the ship's arrival, as there was nowhere for the containers to be stored even if the docks had the facility to actually offload them. As these were the first containers, no docks had any sort of crane or forklift for the loading and unloading; this was all taken care of by the ship, which was equipped with its own crane. Eventually, on the following Saturday, the ship arrived and they managed to get the boxes lifted off. Bob set off for home empty, getting home in one driving shift!

Offered the chance to attend a trailer manufacturer's open day, Bob accompanied his father to Danbury in Essex. Hoynor trailers was demonstrating some of its equipment to prospective buyers. As well as building rigid truck bodies and car transporter trailers, it manufactured tipping

Guy demonstration truck and trailer.

A few of the demonstration vehicles parked together.

trailers but whereas a traditional tipper trailer would tip the body only, Hoynor tipped the entire trailer up to unload the trailer. Trailers also could be ordered with drop sides, which could be folded back in to create a flatbed trailer. It also offered a dual four in line axle tipper for maximum weight allowance. A four in line axle had four wheels spread out across one axle, 11 tonnes per axle.

Sadly, Hoynor went into liquidation in 1969.

The docks in Felixstowe then began to boom with containerized shipping. This lead to a shift in the workload at Carters, and more and more work was sourced to and from the docks. Unaccompanied trailers shipped in from the Netherlands also became a regular source of work as that area of shipping also became big business. Europoort trailers of Hull and the Italian firm Andrea Merzario became regular customers. This was quite far removed from what most of the local drivers were used to! With increasing work from Felixstowe, Carter's haulage became more involved, and grwadually left behind its grassroots of agricultural- and forestry-sourced work. Trucks that were purchased became artics as standard, as the rigids it used to have were becoming obsolete.

In 1966, after returning from a job one day, Bob found all his family around the kitchen table discussing business. Angered by the fact no one had waited for him for his input, he decided to quit the family business there and then, although he finished the week off so they had time to arrange someone else to drive the truck from then on.

SEAWHEEL, BREAKING THE MOULD

IN AUGUST 1966 BOB USED HIS 'JACK THE LAD' APPROACH to get himself a job at a company called Seawheel.

"I had left Carters in the July, and in that month I couldn't find a job for love nor money. My father had put the mockers on me and phoned around all the local companies telling them not to take me on, as I would soon be back working for him with my tail between my legs. Through a very good friend of mine, Mick James, I'd heard that there was possibly a job coming up at Seawheel. So I popped down to their offices to see them. The only problem was that Bill Coulsden, the manager, already had someone lined up for it and told me that sadly there wasn't a vacancy, and he then went out of the office. Fortunately for me, I knew Mary, who was Bill's accountant, very well, and while he was outside she whispered that he was very worried about the man he had lined up and wasn't even sure if he'd turn up or not, and suggested that I ask again. This was on the Tuesday, so I gave it until the Thursday and I went back to see him again.

"'Has this new driver turned up yet, Bill?' I asked.

"Well, that caught him unawares, as he had no idea I knew about the other driver that he'd got lined up!

"He told me he still hadn't heard from him, and so I asked where the truck was. Apparently it was a brand new AEC, and it was awaiting collection from the dealership in Ponders End, North London.

"'In for a penny, in for a pound,' I thought and decided to make him a proposal.

"'If the man hasn't turned up or been heard from by Friday morning,' I said, 'I will collect the truck for free, deliver the load and if he still does not appear, I will get the job.'

I had left Carters in the July, and in that month I couldn't find a job for love nor money.

The only truck Bob ever had brand new, in 1966.

Seawheel's Dodge yard shunter.

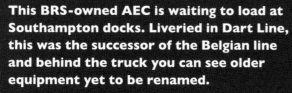

This BRS-owned AEC is waiting to load at Southampton docks. Liveried in Dart Line, this was the successor of the Belgian line and behind the truck you can see older equipment yet to be renamed.

Loading with a straddle carrier at Southampton docks. The Belgian line was the first company to use the new container handling facilities at Southampton docks.

The *Suffolk*, loading up Seawheel containers for continental Europe at Felixstowe docks.

Seawheel only ever had three of its own trucks on the road.

Outside James Bridge copper works, West Midlands. This truck was owned by BRS but liveried in Seawheel colours.

Bob's truck on the quayside.

It was not purely its own containers that Seawheel delivered. A Eurotransport tilt trailer is ready for delivery.

Frank Tovell washing down his truck in Seawheel's yard.

Loaded up for export.

John Weedon's ERF loading an empty container. Due to containers not having built in forklift 'sleeves', the forklift driver got out by leaving a block of wood under the container and then knocking this wood out after the forklift had gone!

"Well, he couldn't really say no to that as the trailer was loaded, ready to go and had to be there.

"I went straight back to Carter's yard, and spoke to Bill Healey, the yard foreman, to see if any trucks were going to London bright and early, and if so could I hitch a ride. Sure enough, one was leaving at about 4am the following morning. Up with the sun, I was in the yard and on my way to the AEC dealership by 4.30am. The old boy dropped me off on the North Circular around 7am and I walked to the dealership, collected the truck and brought it back to Felixstowe. I was almost back at Seawheel's depot when the truck started spluttering, which a brand new truck shouldn't do! I got it back to the yard, and told Bill that the truck wasn't quite 100 per cent right, but I wasn't too sure why.

"'Not to worry,' he said. 'As it's a brand new truck we'll get it sorted under warranty.'

"So I went home, and returned the following morning to see if this other driver had turned up. Lo and behold there hadn't been any word from him. Good old Mary for giving me the lowdown. Bill had no choice but to give me the job!

"I hitched the truck up to its trailer and took it home, a common occurrence back then, and thought I may as well leave on the Sunday as I was delivering first thing Monday morning to somewhere in South Wales. So, as excited as a pig in the proverbial, I drove down Sunday afternoon, parked outside the factory gates and found some digs close by to get a decent night's sleep.

> *I hitched the truck up to its trailer and took it home, a common occurrence back then*

"Monday morning, by nine o'clock I was tipped and rang the office to see if there was a reload. I spoke to Mary and she told me that Bill wasn't in yet but there was a collection booked for my vehicle from Avon Tyres in Melksham the following morning.

"Well, I thought, I had nothing to lose by heading that way and seeing if the load was ready, fortunately it was and by one o'clock I was loaded and ready to roll.

"Up to now things had gone really well but as a new boy I thought I'd better not get a reputation as a 'scrab arse' in my first week of employment and needed to get the 'feel' for how the firm operated. I was well ahead of myself as it was so I decided not to 'bend' any rules and I parked up for the night at a well-known driver's digs, the Royal Oak in Devizes. Tuesday morning, still ahead of the game, I had some breakfast, before climbing back into the truck ready to head back to Felixstowe.

"Turning the key, other than uselessly churning over for a couple of minutes, there was no sign of life, so retrieving my toolkit from under the pile of ropes in the passenger footwell, I tilted the cab and looked to see if I could find the fault.

"Cracking open a couple of the injector pipes with a spanner I found there wasn't any diesel coming through, so I took off the lift pump, dismantling it only to find that the diaphragm had a pinhole in it. 'Ah', I thought, 'that would explain why it was spluttering when I picked it up.'

"Waiting till 9am for Bill to get into the office, I phoned him from the café call box.

"'Bill I've broken down in Devizes,' I said. 'The lift pump has packed up.'

"'How'd you know that Bob?'

"I told him I was looking at it right now!

"Well he hit the roof!

"'That truck is under warranty, what the hell are you doing taking it to pieces!' he yelled.

> *The only other trouble I had was when I nearly broke the thing in half!*

"When he eventually calmed down I told him that the nearest AEC people were in Bristol, and when he spoke to them to make sure to tell them exactly what the problem is. When the fitter turned up, he was stunned.

"'Mate, this is the first time that I have ever been to a breakdown and the driver has told me exactly what I need and haven't had to go back to the depot for more spares or tools!'

"Within about 30 minutes I was ready to roll again and headed back to Felixstowe, and mechanically the truck wasn't any more trouble from that day on.

"The only other trouble I had was when I nearly broke the thing in half!

"I had loaded a heavy consignment of chipboard for Birmingham, quite heavy, but not illegal by any means. Crossing the old bridge at Claydon just outside Ipswich at about 15mph, I heard a bang but I thought it was just the load moving as chipboard was often liable to do. Checking my mirrors and seeing nothing untoward, I carried on with my journey through Stowmarket, to Bury St Edmunds and onwards, parking up at my usual haunt, the Enterprise Café at Madingley, the other side of Cambridge. I would never go past my favourite transport cafe without stopping! Whether coming or going from Felixstowe, I stopped there that often I had a permanent bed in the digs. It got to the point where if they had to give my bed away I would stay with the family themselves in their bungalow!

"I was sat in the café having some food and Vic, who had been on the first Sea Land job with me when I was working for Carters, came in.

"'Bob is that your AEC outside?' he asked.

"Now, being as it was quite a new truck, a lot of people wanted to have a look round it.

"'It certainly is Vic,' I told him proudly.

"'Come and have a look at it,' he offered.

"Well I thought he just wanted to have a look around it. Walking outside, he

John's as yet unliveried Ford D1000. Powered by a V8 Cummins, this truck was to meet a premature end . . .

March 1968. After loading a Seawheel flat container at Round Oak Steel in Brierley Hill, West Midlands, driver Mick Banyard was heading back towards home. Near the village of Bottisham, a German car dangerously overtook another car, causing him to swerve. He hit a Ford Zephyr, splitting that car in two, which broke his track rod and brake valve. Despite his best efforts, he simply could not control it, and the truck actually flipped on to its roof, shooting the load into the road and nearby hedges. Mick was trapped in the cab, and the radiator split, which gave him some serious burns, and with his other injuries, he ended up in Addenbrooke's hospital for sixteen weeks. Incredibly, at the time he had a 'trade plater' in the truck with him, who simply did a runner as soon as he could get out. The accident scene took two full days to clear up as the load was of hardened steel rod, which had become embedded into the road and bent at all sorts of angles.

A Seawheel-liveried S. Jones ERF unloads an empty flat rack after delivery.

S. Jones seen here delivering a consignment to a steel works in the West Midlands. Imported from Germany, it would arrive on the Freightliner train at its new depot in Landor Street, from where Jones would collect it.

Bartrums of Diss Volvo F86 collecting rebar from Ipswich docks.

F. B. Atkins of Derby, seen here in its yard at Finedon, was a regular Seawheel subcontractor.

Loading rebar from Ipswich. Visible are two vehicles of Davisons of Shildon, and also a Leyland Beaver belonging to Pointers of Norwich.

pointed to the chassis just in front of the rear spring hanger. There was a crack on either side about an inch wide! So, once again, I was on the phone to Bill.

"'I can't go any further Bill, I've snapped the truck in half.' That made Bill cough I can tell you!

"I dropped the trailer while he arranged for another tractor unit to carry on with the load.

"Of course, there was a big inquest into how it had happened and I thought I was going to get fired. I spent some time looking around the chassis of the damaged unit and I had also checked a couple of the same make and spec that Carters were running. I noticed that they had flex plates between the fifth wheel and the chassis, and my Seawheel one had them but incorrectly fitted! I pointed this out to Bill, and he tore into the dealership, Arlington Motors, until they eventually backed down, stripped the truck down and replaced the chassis. The truck was only two months old at the time!"

I thought I was going to get fired.

Seawheel only ever had three trucks and six trailers based in Felixstowe, and eventually when they were sold on they were not replaced and all work was sub-contracted out. After two years of driving for the firm, Bill surprisingly tendered his resignation and Bob was offered his job. He asked for time to think about it, as he enjoyed being on the road, but the company was under pressure and asked him to take over temporarily.

Starting as the temporary traffic planner, Bob soon realized he had taken a pay cut as driving offered the potential to earn a lot more money.

The work was all short sea shipping, to mainland Europe and Scandinavia. There were a lot of metal exports, as Shaw Lovell, which owned Seawheel, was one of the biggest metal brokers in Europe. Every day it would handle a train that came up from South Wales loaded with steel for the Volkswagen factories in Germany. It went against what Bob had always known and believed to see freight going on trains. As the business expanded, regular haulage routes became established within the UK. Every night O.J.H. Smith trunked a load of ICI Mond (everything but fertilizer) to Liverpool. When this trunk trailer was full the excess would be loaded on to a Turners (Soham) trailer, which also had a nightly trunk from Martlesham to Liverpool.

Operating from offices in London, C. Shaw Lovell provided Seawheel with quite a lot of its traffic. Eventually, as business grew, it was deemed more feasible

Seawheel loaned
a container for a
demonstration aimed at
getting the overall weight
limits in the UK raised.
It is loaded on a Tasker
trailer coupled to an –
unusual for the time – 6
× 4 Rolls-Royce-powered
Guy tractor unit. The
demonstration took
place at the Freightliner
depot in Dudley.

for the company to have its own office in Felixstowe. Having someone there to deal directly with things such as customs clearance made more sense.

In 1967 it took over a room in Seawheel's office, and a man called Bert Kellard was sent to run the office. The room used was the plushest in the building, and was only meant for board meetings, etc! This set-up proved to work well, and Bob and Bert became firm friends.

Working for the Crown agents, Hogg Robinson, the NAAFI also became a regular customer for Seawheel. Every day containers were loaded from just outside Southampton for the British Army of the Rhine (BAOR) military bases in Germany. Bob would only use his trusted haulier, Bakers of Southampton, for this job. It would load almost every day and bring the loaded box to Felixstowe, returning with an empty for the next day or possibly a loaded one to deliver en route home.

LEP transport from London was another regular client, the difference being that with this customer Seawheel would pull LEP trailers. The main collection point would be just outside Dumfries in Scotland, loading computers for West Germany.

One day, while back in the driver's seat providing some holiday cover and en route to load at yet another regular customer, Melody Wallpaper Mills, Bob had his third and final jackknife of his career!

"It was early one winter's morning, and I wanted to be first in the queue when the mill opened as it used to take a few hours to load a container. Access to the mills was downhill through a residential area, nothing too steep, but still a hill. As I dropped down the slope I had to dab the brakes to back it off a bit and before I knew it the trailer was around at 90 degrees to me! It hit the kerb on my near side and bounced across to the one on the offside. In the distance near the bottom of the hill I could see a milk float parked on the side and was waiting for the impact. The milkman could see what was likely to happen, and had scampered into someone's garden to keep out of harm's way! As my truck loomed down on it, the trailer hit the kerb again, bounced back across to the opposite side, completely missing the milk float, coming to a halt at the bottom of the road, the whole outfit flush to the opposite kerb but facing the wrong way, with the tractor unit within 2in of someone's rear bumper!"

Before I knew it the trailer was around at 90 degrees to me!

It wasn't long before Bob was then promoted to 'Transport Development Manager' for the UK, and into a new office in the Trelawny House building in Felixstowe docks. One of the first customers was The Belgian Line, which soon merged with two other companies, Clarke Traffic of Canada and The Bibby Line of Liverpool. They all become Dart Line, (which today is called OOCL).

The contract with Dart Line started Seawheel's operation out of Southampton. Bob was by now encouraging the concept of hauliers painting their tractor units

Guy Big J4 owned by Aston Clinton Haulage. It is back at Seawheel's yard in Felixstowe having loaded aluminium ingots from the Alcoa factory, which was located close to its operating depot at Aylesbury.

An Ernest Cross AEC loaded with two new 20ft containers, but on to a 33ft trailer. Look at that overhang!

O.J.H. Smith Dodge. Also loaded with two new containers.

Ernest Cross Commer two-stroke, seen loading at Parkeston Quay, Harwich. Imagine trying to walk around a container port nowadays like the gentlemen in the photographs!

George Cooper of Manningtree with his new Scania 110, painted in Seawheel's colours.

Bob didn't hold any bad feelings towards the family company and often gave it work. Here two of its trucks – a Ford D1000 and also a rare 'Chinese six' AEC Mammoth Minor – are seen loading rebar from Ipswich docks.

Carter's Guy Big J4 with Seawheel box.

W. Carter AEC at Felixstowe. Note the unusual wheel combination on the trailer.

Hilton Transport Services (HTS) from Charlton, Seddon, waiting to load a container in Felixstowe.

Subcontractor Lists of Debenham. Behind the wheel is its long-time driver, 'Jock' Wardlaw.

in Seawheel colours for long-term contracts. Contract vehicles that ran trucks in Seawheel colours included: S. Jones (Aldridge), George Cooper, Page Brothers, John Weedon, Hilton Transport Services (HTS), Thomas Allen, and O.J.H. Smith. Non-painted trucks included: BRS, F.B. Atkins of Derby, Lists of Debenham, and Henry Smyther.

Seawheel also had an Irish service, which ran from Avonmouth docks and the much smaller Preston docks, which was situated alongside the River Ribble, an extremely tidal stretch of water.

During his time at Seawheel, Bob struck up a good working relationship with a man called George Gill, who had previously worked for Freightliner but was now working for Seatrain Lines, and one day phoned Bob in a bit of a muddle. He needed a 40ft container taken to Aylesham in Norfolk for loading at two o'clock that same afternoon. Seatrain's current haulier, Reece Transport from London, couldn't cover the job and it simply had to be loaded that day. So Bob phoned around his list of hauliers, but no one could be found to cover it. His last phone call was to a friend who was a farmer and who also owned a truck that did a bit of local haulage now and again. David 'Sloppy' Foster agreed to do the job in his Guy Big J. tractor unit. He had to collect the trailer for the job from Reece's and it was very reluctant to hand the trailer over despite the fact it couldn't cover the job itself, but eventually it relented. Sloppy collected the container from the docks, and was in Aylesham on time for the two o'clock collection. Another favour done. This was the start of a long-term working partnership for Bob and Seatrain Lines.

Two of Frederick Ray of Leighton Buzzard trucks with specially built containers with side doors for car parts from the Vauxhall motors plant at Luton.

O.J.H. Smith ERF. Note the extra pallets loaded at the front of the trailer for delivery en route to the main destination.

Spinks Interfreight from Darlington loading rebar at Ipswich. These consignments of rebar came in from Canada and provided a steady flow of traffic for Seawheel.

Bakers of Southampton. Most of its work for Seawheel was for the NAAFI.

Thomas Allen Scammell Trunker.

Thomas Allen ERF.

Looking like a promotional shot from the Scania brochure, the Scania Vabis was owned by W. & M. Wood of Enfield. It is seen in Seawheel's yard in Felixstowe. Judging by the look of the trailer, it also has aluminium ingots for export from Aylesbury.

LEP transport also provided a steady flow of traffic for Seawheel.

One of the three regular BRS trucks that Seawheel used.

OJH Smith Seawheel liveried ERF.

W. G. Harvey of Stowmarket Scammell Trunker.

TRANS UK, A STEP INTO THE UNKNOWN

TRANS UK WAS STARTED BY BOB out of the back of his Ford Cortina in 1970. He takes up the story . . .

After a disagreement about my worth to Seawheel, I decided to hand my notice in. This came as a shock to the powers that be, who tried to persuade me to stay. Well, as long as the money goes up then I will I told them. However one month turned into another with no sign of the suggested pay rise. This helped me to make up my mind. I didn't want to leave under a cloud or burn by bridges, so I decided to stay on board with them until they found a suitable replacement for me, which in fact turned into two people to do my job."

I knew that I had sufficient contacts to make a go of it as a freight forwarder from what I'd learned at Seawheel but, before I left, I spoke to Bert Kellard at Shaw Lovell to see if he would give me any work if I decided that was the route I was going to take. He agreed that as long as the goods would be delivered on time and not cost the earth, he would give me regular work.

Well this was already how I operated my transport desks, the only difference would be that in future I would be in total control!

"Well this was already how I operated my transport desks, the only difference would be that in future I would be in total control!

"I promised Bert I would only use good reliable subcontractors; there were cheaper people about, but I gave my word the loads would be there on time every time, and do you know what, in the fullness of time, using quality operators, we rarely let people down.

"So, when I left, my company, Trans UK Containers, was born. I chose the name simply because *that* was what I planned on doing, transporting containers around the UK.

"I started by approaching the different clearing houses and shipping agents that I knew in the Felixstowe area to see what work they had to cover, and if they didn't have any work I would at least ask for a cup of coffee to make up for the time wasted! If they had work to be covered, I would then borrow their phones to speak to subcontractors I knew to see if they had a truck available for a back load. Things were a lot more personal back then, and people didn't really go round undercutting the rates, as is the norm these days. The transport industry was run in a much more gentlemanly fashion before the O (operator's) licence was implemented."

Bob had built up a good pool of local hauliers he could rely on, as well as various others from around the country. Being of a non-aggressive character with a sociable personality he found it easy to build personal relationships with the relevant people.

As his business developed, and got progressively busier, he realized that before long he would have to consider purchasing some trucks of his own.

In fact, the very first truck Bob bought was an old AEC Mandator, from truck dealer Percy Nicholls. It was owned previously by Chieftain Yeast of Felixstowe (now British Fermentation Products).

Hand painting the unit himself in his new company colours, Bob actually had a truck 'on the road' before he had an office to work from! The old Mandator was never officially put on an O licence, or taxed for road work, as its intended use was to be solely for shunting containers within the docks. Despite this, Bob would sometimes sneak on to the public road to go to a company called Seavan Pack at the Fisher Terminal off Walton Avenue. All the work this truck did was for an American company called Seatrain Lines, which was the sole shipper and contractor for American forces' personal effects.

Bob would drive the unit at night, shunting and loading normally six Seatrain trailers.

As Bob knew a lot of the tug drivers from his years working in and out of the docks, he would often ask the dockers for their help by loading the odd trailer for him while he was busy shunting others about. He would leave the empty trailer with the container's release form, and for a small price the tug driver would load one of his containers for him. This could save him

Bob would drive the unit at night, shunting and loading normally six Seatrain trailers.

hours in waiting about. Each shunt paid £15, so it was a terrific earner and a nice little backhander for a dock driver. It was a very cost-effective way to keep his business growing and also of satisfying the tug drivers.

By 1971, Bob was employing his old work colleague, Mary. She was working from home, as there was *still* no office. Eventually, after some time searching for suitable premises, he took out a lease on an office and some yard space in C. Shaw Lovell's yard in Sub-Station road, Felixstowe. The work was building up nicely, and he had a good band of subcontractors to do the work for him.

A brochure from good customer Overdorp.

Overdorp's office, which inspired Bob to use an open plan approach to his own offices.

One particularly good customer was a Dutch firm called Overdorp, which shipped its specialized trailers into the UK via another client, Seaspan Freight. It would ship unaccompanied trailers from the Netherlands for delivery in the UK. These would be loaded mainly with a computer card, which the analogue computers of the time required.

Because of the sensitivity of the load and the extreme cleanliness required of the trailers, Overdorp was extremely fussy about any reload Bob could source for it. Most of the time it just wanted its trailers back empty in order to reload them again for the UK. This work was booming, with four or five trailers arriving for delivery every day. It was becoming more and more obvious that Bob would have to purchase trucks of his own to handle the volume of traffic his business was developing.

By 1973, with the workload increasing, only three units on the road, *and* the lease on the office and yard coming to an end, Bob had to start looking once again elsewhere for new facilities.

Finding an office at the Crane Fruehauf building on Dooley Avenue in Felixstowe, a building now long gone and converted into haulage yards, he arranged truck parking at the tobacco bond on the docks.

By now, on any given day, Trans UK Containers could have up to thirty jobs.

With all this going on, Bob had researched what type of tractor units and trailers he should purchase and bravely decided on the relatively untested Volvo F86 matched to Tasker trailers. 'Bravely' because as yet the British haulage industry was still heavily reliant on British-manufactured tractor units with 12-litre engines, crash gearboxes and little in the way of driver comforts. The thought of change was an anathema to most of the old style hauliers. Yet here was Bob Carter about to invest in six 5.9-litre (smaller than many American car engines) 32-ton cap Volvos! Most drivers considered them to be too girlie and not proper trucks at all . . . until they'd had a couple of days behind the wheel and could actually hear the fitted radio.

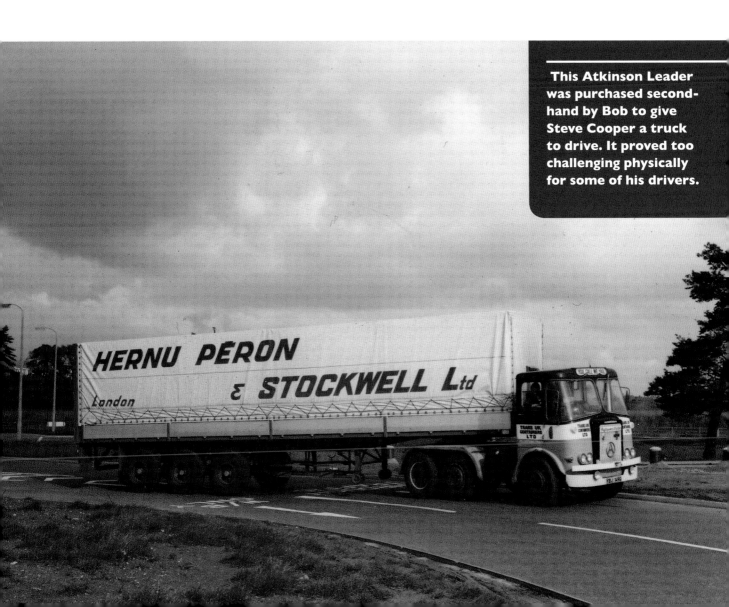

This Atkinson Leader was purchased second-hand by Bob to give Steve Cooper a truck to drive. It proved too challenging physically for some of his drivers.

Advertisement for Trans UK. Note the advertisers of the day have 'doctored' the truck's registration to make it appear a lot newer that it was (a fact none of us had spotted until the other week!).

The complete package of F86 and Tasker trailer proved a win-win for Bob as there was a saving of nearly a ton on the unit alone. Couple that with their inherent reliability and service back-up and it was a great buy, eventually!

With the imminent arrival of the first trucks ordered from Duffields (Volvo) of Norwich at a job lot price of £32,000, a new division was born: Trans UK Haulage Limited.

The first trucks for 'on the road', having been ordered in 1971, finally arrived in 1972!

The problem was, that as Bob was a new customer he wasn't too high on the priority list for receiving his new vehicles. This was a time of rapid expansion at Felixstowe dock as it fought to become one of Europe's biggest and most important container ports and many valued companies such as Ferrymasters that had put in a large order for vehicles at the same time were obviously receiving preferential treatment.

It took almost fifteen months for all of the first of the Trans UK Haulage vehicles to arrive, unthinkable nowadays!

The trailers, bought from Taskers, where Bob knew the salesman well, were sitting waiting for their new horses.

And talking about horses, each tractor unit was to be named after a Dartmoor stallion, while each tilt trailer was named after the wife or girlfriend of an employee or one of the office staff. The trailers were given the prefix 'Mi lady', a nod to the olden day pronunciation given to a lady.

It took almost fifteen months for the first of the Trans UK Haulage vehicles to arrive, unthinkable nowadays!

"The idea was, that the lady, aka the trailer, was sat upon a Dartmoor stallion, or the tractor unit," says Bob. "For example, Mi lady Jilly would be sat upon Cawsand Black Velvet."

When they eventually arrived they were a real mishmash of registrations, and although new, one had an L prefix registration, four were Ms and one was an N reg!

As soon as they were prepared for the road, two of the trucks were put to work on contract to Shaw Lovell, which left only four units to cover the increasing workload.

Bob, realising he still had a shortfall of vehicles to cope with the rapidly increasing volume of work, decided to look for decent second-hand units as he couldn't afford the long lead time needed to buy brand new trucks.

"In fact," said Bob, "one of the first second-hand trucks I bought actually arrived *before* the new Volvos!"

It was an Atkinson Leader 6x2, bought from Nelson Wright of N.T. Wright Transport, Wenhaston.

"I commented to Nelson one day that I hadn't seen his Atki for a while, and he told me that he couldn't find a driver for it and it was just parked in his yard.

"We came to an agreement on a price and the Atki became my first legal road-going truck."

Put on contract to Johnsons Shipping of London, this was double shifted by Ray Rainham and Steve Cooper, delivering United States Lines containers, day and night to Pedigree Petfoods at Melton Mowbray.

While looking for more trucks, a friend of Bob's, who happened to be working in finance, tipped him off about some vehicles that they would be 'snatching' back in the very near future. They were two Volvo F88 290s with sixteen-speed gearboxes. At the time they were the bee's knees in tractor units. Confiding to him who owned the trucks, Bob realized that he knew the owner as he'd done some work for him in the past. Phoning him up, he spoke to him directly and offered to take on the finance on the trucks if he decided he really couldn't afford them any more. Within a couple of days he accepted his offer and the pair agreed a deal, Bob took on the finance and had another two quality trucks to his name.

> *We came to an agreement on a price and the Atki became my first legal road-going truck.*

The Fiat Trucks joined the fleet because one of Bob's regular subcontractors, Mitchell–Rowlands, had the franchise for Fiat tractors. He already had one truck on the road, and had put it on contract to Trans UK, driven by a chap called Mervyn Woollard.

Fiat units were the latest in the growing list of European manufacturers to try to break into the UK market, and Mitchell–Rowlands was one of the first importers in the country with two Italian-spec day cabs, a 619 and a 684. At that time all Italian tractor units were manufactured in right-hand drive due to the inherent dangers of Alpine driving, so they didn't require much work to meet UK build regulations.

Paul Rowlands, who with Bob's encouragement had moved across from Trans UK to Mitchell–Rowlands in the knowledge that Middle East work would soon be on the cards, had been given one to drive and spoke very highly of its capabilities. At the time it had one of the biggest cabs on the market and had a very sound engine, being called the 'Italian Gardner', high praise indeed in those days.

Bob, with his mechanical and technical background, had a thorough look at one and was impressed enough to decide that if the proposed Middle East work took off and became a successful venture he would purchase a few.

The other marque that eventually featured strongly in the fleet line-up was Magirus Deutz. Built in Germany and with an air-cooled engine, Bob would buy these 'Maggies' mainly second-hand from a company called Essex Truck Sales in Easton, near Great Dunmow.

A man called John Parradine was the owner and chief salesman there and he persuaded Bob to give them a try. Being an open-minded type of guy, he did, the idea being to replace the Volvo F86s as and when necessary.

Bob with Tony Waugh in his office at the Crane Fruehauf buildings, Felixstowe.

Bob's long-serving secretary, Mary Giles.

Graham Carter, John Joyce and Tommo the yardman seen here in the operations office inside Shaw Lovell's yard and offices, Felixstowe.

Company Secretary
Colin Hillman behind the
equipment control board.

Seatrain containers
filling up no. 72 park,
Felixstowe docks.
They are all aluminium
lightweight boxes,
meaning customers
could increase their
payload. The company
only operated 40ft
containers until almost
the end of its existence,
when it started to add
20ft containers to its
equipment pool.

The Seatrain Lines
boat M/V Euroliner
discharging at Felixstowe.

One of Bob's Volvo F86s with his Ford Transit doing a promotional shoot one weekend. Steve Cooper is behind the wheel of the Volvo.

Trans UK's longest serving driver was Ray Rainham. Seen here with an Overdorp trailer, Ray became the company's London specialist. No matter how many drops there was on the trailer, Ray would get them all done in a day, and back home again. No one knows quite how he did it, and he just grins when you try and ask him!

Two 'Maggies' at the Routemaster.

A pair of brand new Magirus Deutz liveried in Shaw Lovell's name for regular contract work.
Photo: Bert Kellard

In fact, what happened was that as the units arrived they just ended up extending the fleet, such was the amount of work being garnered by his rapidly expanding company.

The big bonus was their low kerb weight, which allowed for a higher carrying capacity.

Selecting a company colour scheme for the fleet had been a relatively simple task. Influenced by Seawheel's simple yet effective colours, Bob chose black, white, red and grey. Going against the grain, he decided to have the darkest colour at the top, mostly because everyone he'd asked advice from had said that it would be better the other way up!

"Being occasionally cantankerous, I decided to stick to my guns, this was going to be my fleet and this was the colour scheme I wanted! I have always liked black and grey, and the white band around the middle came from my Seawheel connection, I opted for a red chassis to set the cabs' colours off."

As to the catchy slogan, 'you call, we haul', that came from Bob's teenage years, when he first worked for the family firm. Often helping to load sugar beet into the trucks manually, he was occasionally paired with another of Carter's employees, Ronald 'Nipper' Crisp, who insisted on humming while loading, "you call we haul, you call we haul", and it stuck with Bob from that day on . . .

The next few months in early 1975 were spent organizing Trans UK Continental's maiden Middle East run, eventually deciding to send four vehicles, with Bob and transport manager Colin Stayden travelling in convoy in Bob's Humber Sceptre.

The convoy consisted of:

Lenny Balaam driving a Trans UK Volvo F88.

Owner driver Terry Blakesley in a DAF 2800.

Owner driver Bob Crofton-Sleigh in a day cab Fiat 619.

A Mitchell–Rowlands unit driven by Paul Rowlands also in a Fiat 619, but with a sleeper cab.

As with most companies, the work Trans UK did to the Middle East came about through current customers wanting a good reliable service, something Trans UK had proved it could provide in the UK.

Bob continues: "The Bulgarians were doing work for one of my customers, CEP Transport in Felixstowe. Due to ferry costs the Bulgarians wouldn't actually come to England themselves, so we used to unload and load their unaccompanied trailers in England, then ship them back to Holland. The problem was that

A line-up of Fiats at the Routemaster building, Felixstowe. Photo: Gerry Keating

Overdorp was a good customer of Trans UK, with several trailers needing delivery every day throughout the UK.

Trans UK's yard in Sub-Station Road, Felixstowe. One of John Weedon's ERF tractor units is also visible.

Volvo F88 at Felixstowe.

Rupert Solomon's Volvo F86, which he purchased from Bob and then worked as a subcontractor. He was known to everyone as Rupert the bear. The child in the photo is Bob's son James.

Bob's son James behind the wheel of the Atkinson Leader.

Maggie in Felixstowe.
Photo: Gerry Keating

they never knew where the trucks were, they were often late and when they transited Bulgaria the driver would often go home! So if they didn't do another trailer change the load could sit there for a week before continuing on its journey!

"Colin Stayden, their transport manager, was complaining to me one day about his lack of control on delivery times when using Bulgarian operators, and I responded by saying that *we* could do the run, but I wasn't just going to send the one truck, I would send a number! I also said I would personally go with the trucks on the first trip, to oversee it.

"His immediate response was: 'Well in that case, I'm going to come with you!'

"Well that was agreed then! The only problem was that, even though I was more than happy to sleep in a car or a truck, Colin was more used to a life of luxury, so to speak, and a night in a hotel would have been the norm."

"'Sleeping in a car, you're bloody joking!' exclaimed Colin when I talked of my plans.

"He had always been an office-based man, and on the trip this caused a bit of friction, but I managed to keep him happy with a mix of hotels and the car."

As already recounted, the first trip was undertaken in four trucks. One of Trans UK's own, and three subcontractors, including one who was driving a day cabbed Fiat!

'Sleeping in a car, you're bloody joking!' exclaimed Colin when I talked of my plans.

Bob Crofton-Sleigh and Terry Blakesley were loaded for Tehran out of LEP Packing in Chiswick, and Lenny Balaam and Paul Rowlands were loaded with various smaller consignments, 'groupage', for several different customers that were all going to be delivered to a distribution centre in Abadan docks.

The whole kit and caboodle shipped out of Felixstowe for Zeebrugge on 1st June 1975, cleared customs and set off for West Germany and the freight train at Eifeltor on the outskirts of Cologne that would take the trucks south to Ludwigsburg. Disembarking from the train in the early hours, the convoy headed for Munich, Austria and Yugoslavia.

Line-up at the Routemaster, Felixstowe.

The journey down through the rest of Europe was pretty uneventful.

One thing Bob specifically noticed was that no Western-owned truck would go past another one that had broken down at the side of the road. Even drivers from the likes of Hungarocamion, (the Hungarian state-owned transport company) would stop and help out.

All the while, Bob was making notes about distances, times, road conditions, forms that needed to be filled out at the numerous borders, monies that needed to be paid and all the many other ancillary bits and pieces of information needed to ensure successful future trips.

"I wanted to put together a booklet for my drivers to equip them for when we started running the Middle East route properly, to try and make their job as easy as possible when dealing with the various borders and situations," Bob explains.

The convoy crossed into Turkey through the Bulgarian border at Kapitan Andreevo–Kapikule on 6th June. This was a border already notorious for long delays, but luckily enough on this first trip the customs formalities on both sides were completed in about four hours.

Lenny in his Volvo loading on to the ferry in Felixstowe.

From left to right.
Unknown, Lenny Balaam,
Bob Crofton-Sleigh,
Paul Rowlands and Terry
Blakesley.

Lenny gives his truck one last look before the train journey starts.

The blue Volvo seen here was owned by a fellow Brit, and its journey would shadow the Trans UK trip. Bob would even help repair its Scania.

Salzburg border into Austria. Note the Scania owned by A. Dowell, another company from Suffolk.

The parking area at Salzburg. The Scandinavian Volvo F89 possibly would have had some issues with the height of his load if he was heading to the Gulf. Also note the Stouff Berliet, a French company that was a common sight on the road to the Middle East.

Coming off part of the new motorway section in southern Austria. This new motorway network was being developed by the Austrians to replace their single lane roads, which were commonly known by truck drivers as the Ho Chi Minh trail.

Another day, another queue! The trucks join the back of the queue and await the clearing agents' young kids, who collected their paperwork and then started the process of clearing the trucks. In Trans UK's case this was the – now internationally renowned – Young Turk.

Queuing at the Yugoslavian–Bulgarian border at Dimitrovgrad.

"While the lads were having their carnets and other paperwork dealt with I took the opportunity to introduce myself to Mehmet, known as Young Turk, who would be doing all our future customs clearances at Kapicule. A pleasant, efficient young man with the added bonus that his father was the customs chief at the border!

"I allowed the lads a day off at Londra Camping (the Mocamp) in Istanbul before continuing our journey across the mountainous landscape of Turkey. This day off halfway through the trip became a regular, encouraged stop-off, as in our view the drivers would benefit from a rest day in either direction."

Crossing Turkey, things seemed to be going all too well, until Bob had an incident in his car.

"We were driving between Sivas and Erzincan at the front of our little convoy when I hit a railway line rather hard.

Paul Rowlands, who was following about 100 yards behind, takes up the tale.

"We were driving across one of the few flat sections of the Anatolian plateau with mountains raised either side in the distance. Bob and Colin were doing maybe 60 to 65mph. As I passed a railway crossing warning sign I suddenly saw the old Humber bounce in the air and come crashing down, the roof rack taking off, bouncing off the roof of the car only to come crashing down on the side of the road, disgorging its contents into the dusty verge. It was like watching a cartoon in slow motion. Pulling up in time to stop the same disaster befalling us, we all piled out to help."

We were driving between Sivas and Erzincan at the front of our little convoy when I hit a railway line rather hard.

Time for tea! The convoy takes a break near Dragoman, Bulgaria.

Waiting on the Bulgarian border with Turkey at Kapitan Andreevo, the trucks would proceed through what was known as 'the sheep dip' and onwards to the Turkish customs.

Bob continues the story: "Such was the impact of hitting the crossing at speed it had caused the luggage rack to dent the roof of the car sufficiently to require a little amateur bodywork attention. So while the boys straightened out the slightly misshapen roof rack, me and Colin climbed inside the car to give the roof a bit of a kick to return it to an almost 'as new' state before refitting the rack and strapping on our now worse for wear luggage! Having a look at the railway crossing, we noticed that the infill between the actual lines was mostly missing! How the suspension wasn't seriously damaged I'll never know."

The rest of the journey across the Anatolian Plateau went without further mishap. Even the crossing of the infamous Tahir mountain with its associated stories of stone throwing children and supposed 'bandits' came to nothing. Mind you, the stories obviously had a negative effect on some travellers, as while parked at Horosan for a short break, the convoy was approached by five English lads driving a Land Rover. They were en route to Delhi and asked if they could join the small group over the 9,000ft pass! Explaining that they were likely to be suffocated by the accompanying dust clouds, Bob said of course, and suggested they follow the first truck as it moved out. A day later, having successfully crossed the mountain, they found themselves at the Turkish–Iranian border, Gurbulak–Bazargan.

A major problem with driving in Turkey is the seemingly continuous battle 'foreign' drivers seem to have with Turkish commercial vehicle drivers.

A major problem with driving in Turkey is the seemingly continuous battle 'foreign' drivers seem to have with Turkish commercial vehicle drivers. Known colloquially by West European drivers by the epithets 'Tonka', due to their similarity to children's toy lorries produced at the time, and 'Kamikaze', for the bus drivers and their particularly 'uninhibited' style of driving.

Tonkas are a four- or six-wheeler rigid lorry, often petrol driven, usually underpowered and almost always horrendously overloaded, that criss-cross Turkey in their thousands.

These Tonka trucks were a bane in the life of international lorry drivers as they would often sneak alongside the long queues of lorries at the borders and if they saw even a smidgen of a gap would try and push their way in, and once in would then allow their mates to also push in. Woe betide you if you happened to doze off in the queue, because when you woke up you could guarantee there would be trucks in front of you that were not there when you nodded off, it was a case of everyone for themselves.

In 1975 this was not a 24/7 border, closing at ten o'clock at night and opening at 7am, which meant that you could at least get some sleep without fear of losing your place. Bob's little convoy arrived at the back of a short queue mid-afternoon, and after submitting their paperwork to the Deugro agent, were finally able to enter Iran twenty-four hours later.

Bob Crofton-Sleigh in his day-cabbed Fiat about to resume a long slog east after a short break near Yozgat.

Tahir pass.

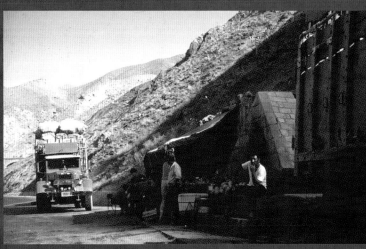

A view of the stark beauty of the Anatolian plateau, somewhere between Zara and Imranli.

Stopping for some fresh supplies in Turkey, they were soon joined by this 1950s era Iranian-registered Mack.

Fuelled up and finished for the day. Time for an 'Efes Kontrol!' Between Erzincan and Erzurum.

Bob Crofton-Sleigh on Tahir.

Bob Crofton-Sleigh crossing Tahir. Behind in the photo you can see a British-registered Land Rover, which contained five young men from England who were heading overland to India. They did not want to cross Tahir on their own after hearing all the 'horror' stories so they asked if they could join the Trans UK convoy.

Getting ready to overtake two heavily laden Greek registered Mercedes before the proper climb of Tahir started.

Two Greek-owned Mercedes climb Tahir.

Lenny and Bob on Tahir.

Paul Rowlands 'blazing the trail' on the drop down Tahir.

Ascending Tahir from the Horosan end.

The long winding descent of Tahir to Eleskirt.

Lunchtime! Stopped on the plateau near Refahiye.

East of Sivas, the convoy takes a break to have a bath in the river Kizilirmak, which means Red river in Turkish, which flows alongside the road.

Bath time! Bob cleans some of his road dust off and has some quality time with the boys!

The Iranian side of Bazargan border.

Bob's Humber at Bazargan. Seen in the photo is Colin Staydon, from CEP transport. Also behind his car is a used Scottish-built Albion cement mixer, being driven overland from the UK to start a second life in Iran. How hardcore is that!

A Turkish Ford D series finally rolls out of the customs pound and heads into Iran. Note the diesel tank lying abandoned on the floor.

The trucks are now parked on the Iranian side of the border but are still awaiting paperwork.

The queue up the hill at Bazargan border.

Bazargan queue.

The queue at Bazargan.

Once into Iran, Paul and Lenny headed into Maku to have some running repair work done on their diesel tanks. The restraining straps holding their tanks in place had moved due to the incessant vibration and flexing of the chassis. This was caused by the horrendous road conditions prevalent while transiting Turkey.

Once the repairs were completed, they all headed south, parking for the night in a dusty off-road area that constituted 'the Oasis' café lorry park, about halfway between Maku and Marand. After a partially edible meal based around some type of meat and a couple of atrocious beers, the lads all retired to bed and early the following morning moved out, heading for Takestan, 300 miles away, where the party was due to go their separate ways.

"South of Zandjan we came across a couple of drivers from the Manchester area whose own journey had been shadowing our group's. In fact, they had been on the same train as us when we left Eifeltor. Their Scania appeared to have broken down," recalls Bob.

Being a fitter and a man with generosity of spirit to spare, Bob and the lads set to work in the arid scrubland, helping to strip down the engine.

Bob continues the story: "It was discovered that number six piston had been holed. Over the next few hours this was removed, the engine rebuilt and fired up. Unfortunately, I had forgotten to block off the oil ways to number six cylinder, so the sump became pressurized with the excess oil pouring through where that piston had been. Stripping it down once again, I rectified the fault, before firing it back up. Running on five cylinders it sounded like a bag of spanners being shaken, bloody horrendous, however this was good enough for them to get the ailing truck to the Davis Turner compound in Tehran."

Bob realized that the repairs they had done on the Scania would probably not get it back to the UK, so it was decided in discussion with the two lads that once he'd completed various business meetings he'd lined up with potential customers, he'd assist them in getting their vehicles tipped before recovering the 'injured' one back to the UK on Bob Crofton-Sleigh's stripped down trailer. The other driver, his running partner, took the Scania unit on the back of his Volvo F88.

Both of Bob's loaded trucks bound for Tehran, driven by Bob Crofton-Sleigh and Terry Blakesley, were unloaded and ready for the homeward journey on 14th June, just two weeks after shipping out of Felixstowe. So far everything was running to the pre-planned schedule.

Meanwhile, the other two, Lenny and Paul, once the Scania had been rebuilt, pressed on towards the Gulf and the Port of Abadan, a further 600 miles to the south.

"The drive down to Abadan was pretty uneventful, but with the bonus of stunning scenery and perfectly smooth tarmac roads," said Lenny, "and after dropping out of the hills on to the desert-like floodplain we stopped for the night at a truck pull in near Ahvaz, about 80 miles north of Abadan.

"Complimenting ourselves on getting here on our own, with a glass or two of beer, we started chatting to a local truck driver who spoke fluent English. All of a sudden, two men came into the restaurant and all hell broke loose as they started arguing loudly with the owner. Then things took a turn for the worse as one of the assailants took a knife out of his pocket and cut the owners tie off from behind the knot! My God! We sat there petrified, staring at the ruckus, when the Iranian driver whispered not to say a word and simply look the other way. Then, to add to the chaos, out of the blue, an army vehicle skidded to a halt outside in a cloud of dust and within a few minutes, with the aid of batons and 'gentle' violence, they calmed things down and had taken all, including the restaurant owner, into custody."

Then things took a turn for the worse as one of the assailants took a knife out of his pocket and cut the owners tie off from behind the knot! My God!

The stricken Scania has made it to Tehran and delivered his load.

Filling her back up with oil after Bob's repair.

Back at the new customs compound. This was the last photo Bob took on the trip as shortly afterwards he had his camera stolen.

Bob's truck loaded for home.

Having a well-earned beer after getting the empty trailer loaded on to Bob Crofton-Sleighs truck.

Loading the Scania into the back of his friend's trailer.

Both truck and trailer loaded and secured for home.

"Best not to ask too many questions," said our friendly truck driver.

"To say the least," said Lenny, "we were a little unsettled!"

Meanwhile, back in Tehran. "I found my car was attracting a considerable amount of attention," said Bob. "As it was a top of the range Humber Sceptre, with a 1725cc twin carb engine, walnut dash and an overdrive gearbox, everyone seemed keen to purchase it. The reason for the interest, of course, was that Rootes Group, in an arrangement with the Shah of Iran's government, had agreed to build a huge factory in the country to build the Hillman Minx, the 'run of the mill, common or garden' version of my Humber. Known as the 'Peykan', it was the most common sight on Iranian roads.

"Now, unbeknown to me at the time, unlike the trucks, my car's registration number had not been added to my passport, so I *could* have sold it for a pretty packet and flown home!

"I was also hoping there would be time to go down to Abadan once all the meetings and customs clearances were taken care of, but in the end that idea

The customs compound at Tehran, and the mad scramble to leave. Note the two Hungarocamion trucks, once a common sight all around Europe.

Tehran 'new' customs. What an eclectic mix of vehicles from all corners of Europe and beyond. From left: Scania 110, Hanomag Henschel, Fiat/OM, Mercedes, Bussing and various other models.

didn't come to fruition as both Lenny and Paul were cleared and unloaded very quickly. They were instructed to head back to the Londra camping in Istanbul and telex our Felixstowe office for further instructions.

"As this was our inaugural trip there were no plans to reload the trucks." says Bob. "I wanted to see how the show went and to check on the viability and administrative problems that might be thrown up before attempting it."

Paul and Lenny, having reached Istanbul in double quick time, had been instructed to run back to Graz in Austria, where they met up with Bob, and together were invited to Helmut Heid's rather nice house in the suburbs for a typical Austrian tea . . . huge! Helmut was a new customer for Bob; he was a freight forwarder who he had met on the way down, and provided the customs clearance for the trucks en route. The two men quickly built up a rapport, and Helmut said that it would be no trouble for him to arrange loads back to the UK for the trucks should Bob need it. Sure enough, true to his word, he had loads available when the ensemble arrived back in Austria.

"You call– we haul!"

Trans UK Haulage is looking for trade to the Middle East

Bob Carter at home with thoroughbreds; representing both types of horse power

Trans UK Containers Ltd. and its associated companies, Trans UK Haulage Ltd. and Trans UK Continental Ltd., are the brain children of Bob Carter, their 36 year old chairman and managing director, whose name suggests (quite accurately) that his family had an early start in the transport industry of East Anglia. He is a son of Leslie Carter, head of W. Carter Haulage Ltd. of Melton, which began with a horse and cart. Although the two concerns operate independently of one another, Bob Carter is highly appreciative of the grounding he received in his father's firm.

No favours

Enjoying no favours, he started as a 15 year old tea boy in the office, learning the complex procedures that go into the good administration of a competitive haulage business. He later served three years in the Royal Electrical and Mechanical Engineers and took part in preparations for seven nuclear tests at Christmas Island. Bob Carter returned to Melton as a long distance lorry driver, then broadened his experience still further with Seawheel, climbing the ladder from driver until his appointment as the company's UK transport development manager. He founded Trans UK Containers at Felixstowe in January 1971, and the port remains the principal base for this and the sister companies, all under the umbrella of Trans UK Holdings Ltd.

Trans UK Containers deals with administration, accounts and customer contact for a wide range of domestic work; UK road and rail coverage, including long distance journeys and local haulage from Freightliner terminals, smalls, ex-ship deliveries and general haulage consultancy. Trans UK Haulage Ltd. looks after the operation and maintenance of a fleet of vehicles that comprises eight Volvos (FA 86s and F 88s) and an Atkinson six wheeled unit for the specialist transport of 32 ton loads; 18 trailers range from 20 foot skeletals to 40 foot platform skeletals. Trans UK Continental Ltd., founded in January this year, copes with the international side. In this division is a weekly groupage service, with driver accompanied West German vehicles, between the Ruhr and Felixstowe, London and Manchester. There are also weekly groupage links with Holland, Belgium, France and Italy and full loads direct to consignees' premises. Deep sea departures pose no

problems; frequently the connections can be made within the Haven ports.

Another company in the group is probably the best known, despite the fact that it does no trading in the accepted sense. This is You Call We Haul Ltd., formed to protect the slogan seen on all its vehicles. "It was a phrase thought up by 'Nipper' Crisp at Melton," Bob Carter explains. "He and the late Les Ruddock, transport manager at that time, taught me a great deal about haulage that will never be out dated." His own transport manager at Felixstowe is another professional, John Scott, and the same can be said of fellow director Tony Waugh, company secretary Colin Hillman and traffic operators John Joyce and Graham Carter. Colin Hillman and pioneer employee Mrs. Mary Giles are responsible for all accounting and administration in the group.

Most of the work is, of course, concerned with driver accompanied transport of containers throughout Britain and Western Europe, but Bob Carter is looking further afield to the Middle East. Indeed, he spent the whole of May discovering first hand the potential of Iran and other Gulf nations. His vehicles already range north to Norway and south to Greece and Bob Carter believes that engineering equipment and consumer goods can be profitably handled over the improving network of Middle Eastern roads. He is personally surveying routes and prospects before he commits the group.

Mission to Iran

Bob Carter has recently returned from a fact finding mission to Iran with four of his laden trailers. "People do get into trouble on this route because they fail to plan the whole operation properly", he says. "The calibre of the driver is of the utmost importance. We pay them £500 for a round trip that can be made comfortably within 28 days, then give them a week off". His Trans UK group is sending three trailers a week to Iran by way of the Felixstowe to Zeebrugge link of Townsend Thoresen and overland through Belgium, West Germany, Austria, Jugoslavia, Bulgaria and Turkey. "80 per cent of the problems that arise ought to have been foreseen", he declares. "The cowboy operators and the

failures have received a lot of publicity, but they form a small minority of the traffic.

"We have a good system of agents to help us do more business. On my return journey we back loaded in Austria with chemicals, having taken machinery and groupage out to Iran. Yes, we can make a profit by using trailers on no more than eight round trips. Our mechanical problems have not been serious. The water pump on one of our Volvo units had to be replaced in Ankara, where the service was first class. He considers that Iranian main roads are every bit as good as their equivalent in Great Britain, but describes the highway from Ankara to the border as "diabolical". His vehicles average ten days to Tehran and twelve to Abadan.

RHA Chairman

Bob Carter is serving his second year as chairman of the Ipswich Sub-Area of the Road Haulage Association and has acquired deep knowledge of the many issues facing the industry. One of the worst problems, he says, is the circulation of "dodgy" permits within EEC countries. "There has been a tightening up of the fraudulent aspect and we welcome that as a step towards the easing of restrictions on *bona fide* hauliers."

At home on Lattinford Hill, Capel St. Mary, his wife Sara breeds Welsh Mountain and Dartmoor ponies; that is why his traction units bear the names of famous show jumpers and Dartmoor stallions instead of numbers. In addition to HP greater than the animal variety, the mechanical collection is entirely radio controlled through the Securicor network. Goods-in-transit insurance under CMR and RHA conditions allow *all* goods to be carried, including highly expensive items such as whisky and perfumes.

Most valuable load carried by the group was £250,000 worth of platinum from London to Liverpool. Perhaps the most priceless were items returned to the British Museum from the United States. In its first 14 months the group achieved a turnover of £89,500 for 2,600 loads; in its second year £122,200 for 3,460; in its third £203,000 for 3,600; and in 1974 £320,000 for 4,250.

forty one

Bob pictured outside his house with two of his Volvo tractor units, along with two of the stallions they were named after.

The following day, the drivers collected a load apiece from Weiner Neustadt for delivery back in the UK. This also in turn created a long-standing working partnership between the two companies.

The entire trip from start to finish, as per Bob's original plan, was completed in twenty-eight days. It really could not have been more successful.

With the success of the first trip, the workload to the Middle East expanded rapidly. Trans UK started a regular groupage run from London to Tehran for LEP transport, with a truck departing almost weekly on that job alone. The majority of the work was to Iran, although they would turn their hands to any destination. Bizarrely, and talk about taking coals to Newcastle, there was even a load of carpets delivered overland to Kuwait. 'Smudger' Smith took the load but, unfortunately for Trans UK, payment for the job was never received, so that was the end of that potentially nice little earner.

The type of loads they were delivering were as diverse as was possible, everything from huge cold store doors to oil pipeline machinery. There were two loads of cement mixers delivered to Amman in Jordan, by Mick Prigg, and Mick Coombes. Very little work was turned down.

"If it paid the rate, we'd give it a go," laughs Bob.

The only Trans UK driver to deliver to Iraq was Pete Ransome, who took several loads of white resin from the Shell Chemical works in Ormston, near Manchester, for a freight forwarder called Redwing International. As successful as this job was, however, Peter did run into difficulty on one particular trip. One of the drums on his load had started weeping and was slowly seeping through the trailer floorboards. During the long trip down to Iraq this had left his trailer chassis, and even the back end of his unit, coated in the white resin. Upon his return to the UK, the mechanics tried everything they could think of to remove the compound, but to no avail! It was like concrete, well and truly stuck on, and everything that could be replaced had to be, including most of the trailer's floorboards and various pipework on the tractor unit.

If it paid the rate, we'd give it a go.

Another large customer was Davis Turner, with a weekly groupage departure from its Battersea depot to the port of Piraeus in Greece.

Successfully completing numerous loads without fault, Davis Turner then offered Trans UK the opportunity of Middle East work, which after much deliberation Bob decided not to take on. He felt it was a very controlling company that liked to dictate how the trucks did the run. This was something Bob was not too keen on, preferring his drivers to make their own decisions as to how they completed the job. He was aware by this time that he had an extremely efficient, reliable and loyal set of drivers who knew the job and its pitfalls inside out. Not once, in six years of overland work, sometimes as far afield as Pakistan, were any of his lorries left to rot in the baking Middle East sun, a sign of the professionalism

THE PRACTICABILITY of double-manning vehicles to the Middle East is being considered by Ipswich sub-area's chairman, Mr Bob Carter, of Trans UK Continental, whose mastery of documentation and planning necessary for the overland journey to Iran made a notable impact at the Ailsa Truck symposium in late August (ROAD WAY, September).

Here, it seemed, was a thorough individual who tried to anticipate every contingency. Yet he remained vulnerable, as was evident after the symposium when he returned to his depot at Felixstowe. There he met problems of a type that had been very much under review that day, the same problems that have bedevilled the haulage industry for many years — rate-cutting and complete disregard for an undertaking to provide a stated amount of traffic.

Terrible Turk

All too often in such cases a neighbouring haulier has proved to be the guilty party. In this case, however, it was a shipping and forwarding agent who had backed out of the arrangement, having found a Turkish haulier who apparently was prepared to cut the price to the bone to obtain a return load. Quoting £500 less than Trans UK Continental were being paid, the Turks certainly presented a problem, one that had to be tackled immediately because already the traffic had stopped flowing.

The action came as a shock because the agreement on the number of loads and the rate was no casual arrangement but had followed several approaches by the agent to Trans UK Continental to extend their activities and handle this particular traffic. Eventually it was arranged that four outfits would be sent on a pilot run to Iran, two of them on the 3,500-mile journey to Teheran and two on the 4,000-mile route to Abadan. Mr Carter and a representative of the agents accompanied them, logging and costing accurately the whole journey, which took 10 days to Teheran and 12 to Abadan.

Left in the lurch

The outcome was agreement that three trailers would be sent weekly to Abadan, the undertaking being to provide the traffic until the end of the year to give Trans UK a reasonable time to recoup their considerable initial outlay. The possibility of the traffic building up even to five or six trailers a week had been discussed.

Having committed themselves in good faith, Trans UK faced serious problems because of the sudden

Trans UK Haulage give full publicity to their Middle East overland service with a red and white bumper line along the Volvo. In this illustration a longer-standing aspect of the company's operation is featured—trailer haulage for Overdorp of Holland.

DOUBLE-MANNING TC

cancellation. Steps were taken to try to preserve, or at least salvage, something from the agreement and to look for other traffic while longer-term policy was being considered.

Fortunately, although numbered among the relative newcomers on the road to the Middle East and enjoying what had appeared to be security of traffic, Mr Carter had not lost sight of the fact that competition could only become keener and that the bubble might burst within five years or so. Without waiting for that to happen he had already begun to consider how things might be consolidated and the possibility of saving time by double-manning had occurred to him. The emergency merely speeded up a planned costing operation on these lines.

He has in mind a transit time of eight to nine days to Teheran or 10 days to Abadan instead of 14 at present, compared with the 21 days that the Turkish hauliers are likely to take.

Double-manning would cost £6,000 a year more in wages and insurance. There would be extra running costs. On the credit side the vehicle could be used for three, perhaps four, extra journeys and it is thought that the increased productivity would justify the extra outlay. Rates, it is hoped, would be held at present level, or perhaps increased by around £150. The aim would be to get as much traffic as possible direct from the exporter, who already is likely to be paying a forwarder more than £150 above the haulier's present rate.

The bait for the exporter would be speed and direct control throughout

at no extra cost. The appeal to the driver, especially the family man, would be absences from home reduced to three weeks instead of five weeks, yet his income and time off over the year would be the same.

Current thinking is that two men sharing a cab under the testing conditions experienced on trips to Iran would produce a clash of temperaments. Recent single-bunk cab designs are in line with this thinking. Mr Carter, however, believes that double-manning could work if the driver was allowed to select his own mate and that the team were confident that they could live together on the road for three weeks at a time.

"Two drivers would be as eager as the operators to get the vehicle back to the UK, rather than sit around a foreign lorry park," he says. "Under Common Market regulations they could drive for 16 hours in a day in two eight-hour periods and get from Belgium to Austria in four driving periods. A further 24 hours would see them across Yugoslavia and they could be in Istanbul in three days instead of five days as now. Additional savings would be achieved on the remainder of the journey.

"It has been said that customers will not pay for such a service but we take the view that everyone will be happy about shorter transit times and customers who have been approached about the idea have shown interest and are giving our proposals consideration."

Despite the current happenings Mr Carter accepts that there is a role in transport for reliable shipping and forwarding agents and he has many

26

Trans UK looked into the possibility of double manning on the Middle East run. Photo: The Road Haulage Association dealings with them. He is experienced in most aspects of transport, having grown up in a family haulage business and done most jobs from tea boy to driving the first 32-tonner in the district.

After that he joined Seawheel, rising to UK transport development manager in that organisation and establishing a chain of 18 Seawheel/Dart container depots based on the Freightliner network.

In 1970, with assistance from his brother-in-law, John Weeden, who also had his own haulage business, Mr Carter started Trans UK Containers, initially as a clearing-house operation. Most of the traffic was sub-contracted to local hauliers at Felixstowe: "I knew them all," he says.

From the outset he was involved with shipping and forwarding agents,

only from the UK. A strong trade developed in shipping unaccompanied trailers to Europoort from where, usually unbeknown to the exporter, the goods were transhipped and Eastern European operators took over the transport to the Middle East. The UK trailers, in turn, were reloaded in Holland. Mr Carter speaks from personal experience of this aspect of the trade but believes that the volume is lessening — perhaps because rates are now lower here.

G. A. PEARSON gains from Bob Carter, of Trans UK Continental, some ideas on how haulage to the Middle East could be stabilised

and that what this company is doing in a small way is the type of activity that is needed.

"We believe that what we do is distinctive. In addition to our own fleet we have an arrangement with some locally based small hauliers and a few owner-drivers to provide a licensed vehicle and driver to go to the Middle East. We do the rest, providing the loaded, sealed trailer at our Felixstowe depot and all documentation, including vehicle insurance under which the tractors are added to our fleet policy for the journey. We supply the green card, and, of course, a folder of instructions for the driver identical to that issued to our own men."

All on-costs met

Trans UK obtain and pay for permits, although these are made out in the sub-contracting haulier's name. All carnets and bonds are also provided. The effect is that all on-costs, other than drivers' wages and running costs, are met by Trans UK and deducted from the rate paid to the haulier.

BEAT RATE-CUTTING

C. Shaw Lovell and Sons, and the relationship has flourished unbroken to the extent that Trans UK now have vehicles on contract hire to Shaw Lovell. Growth has been rapid and under what is now Trans UK Haulage Ltd are two operating wings, the domestic Trans UK Containers Ltd and the international Trans UK Continental Ltd, the fleets running on a single O licence for 15 vehicles and 25 trailers.

Operations include groupage within the EEC, this involving the use of depots of agents in London and Manchester. Liaison has also been established with foreign hauliers, including a German company, the co-operation permits that are available from this link having been invaluable for crossing Germany on the way to the Middle East.

Overall, mainly to cope with the many kinds of document necessary in different countries, Trans UK would prefer to work with reliable shipping and forwarding agents rather than deal direct with every exporter. But they say that satisfactory agents are so few that they are being forced to get the traffic direct in order to obtain an equitable rate. Too many agents apparently take the view that the haulier exists purely to be beaten down to a price that will show a further profit to add to the initial commission. Rates being offered from Teheran range from £2,400 to £2,800 yet the higher figure is said to be at least 10 per cent too low for satisfactory haulage.

Competition has become fierce. There are many East Europeans prepared to back-load at a low rate, not

A plastic-sleeved document wallet covering every phase of the Middle East operation is issued to all drivers and is displayed by Bob Carter. Behind him are Rentco trailers used by the company.

We discussed the proposed haulage conference line to the Middle East, or perhaps an RHA co-operative taking on the work, as an alternative to agents. "The conference idea was good," he said, "but there might be a tendency to take any price offered and again pin the haulier down. On the other hand, if the rates were fixed correctly and there was a middle man operating on that scale, the exporter would then be paying high for the service.

"It could be that the industry should be left to work its own co-operative

Although it is sub-contracting to a degree, Trans UK retain control and there is no question of a load being further sub-contracted. The permit cannot be transferred legally. Because of the overheads involved, about £1,600 a vehicle being committed in advance, contracts are for a year's work, or about eight trips.

The main need that Mr Carter sees is for exporters and hauliers to be brought closer together. "Still there would be room for the forwarder to group the traffic if the rate was right — but overall I feel that this Middle East job is mainly an exporter/haulier operation," he says.

Guide needed

Exporters, he believes, should be able to obtain a list of reputable international operators and full details of the services that they offer. Such a list should be publicised and this would enable exporters to keep down costs by looking around instead of placing everything with an agent.

Suggesting that an organisation such as the RHA might produce the list, he adds that Trans UK would be prepared to contribute to the cost. "It would be a reasonable expenditure, whereas even if we operated 25 vehicles on a Middle East service we would not be big enough to carry out an individual marketing operation," he adds.

Stories of disaster on the road to the East have made many headlines.

This way of working, however, never came to fruition.

with which the company was run and the respect in which Bob and his office staff were held by the drivers.

In 1976 a very important reload contract was negotiated with a client called Jimmy Attias, an importer from Guildford in Surrey.

Full loads of pre-boxed bicycles were collected from Sarajevo and Ljubljana, in what was then Yugoslavia, and delivered back to the UK.

If loaded correctly, 408 boxes could be squeezed into the 12m trailers and the volume of work grew so rapidly that Trans UK would often subcontract loads out to Davis Turner and other customers.

"In fact, the work became so prolific, we stopped looking for any sort of reload from the Middle East or Turkey at all," said Bob. "These bicycles became our staple back load. It was a very well-paid job and, due to the cargo being light, it meant that the trucks performed well on fuel as well, a double bonus."

In fact, the work became so prolific, we stopped looking for any sort of reload from the Middle East or Turkey at all

In their continual search for new work and growth, contact was made with Ian Dale, a tractor importer from Gilberdyke, near Hull, that imported regular loads of tractors and small crawlers from the Universal Tractor Company in Brasov, Romania. An agreement was reached and a successful business co-operation was established with many loads collected and delivered to his Hull base. Lacking a bit in quality control but cheap, they were basically an obsolete Fiat tractor built under licence. Almost all of these would go to Hull.

A local man called John Tuffan became one of Bob's best customers. Trading as Didem Exporters, he was half Turkish, and lived just outside Woodbridge, close to Bob. He approached Trans UK about delivering some second-hand tractors to Istanbul. Turkish agriculture at this time was still very 'biblical' in its practical application, with seed still being cast by hand from a hip sack, and they were ready for 'new technology'. Naturally, Bob agreed to give it a try. Four second-hand Massey Ferguson 35 tractors would be loaded into a tilt trailer and sent to Istanbul. The trip went without a hitch, and this workload soon increased.

Bob's yardman at the time, Bryon 'Thommo' Thompson, soon figured out that he could get five tractors into a trailer by removing certain parts and reconfiguring the load. As they were being paid by the tractor this was good news. Eventually, by taking wheels off and loading them at certain angles, he managed to squeeze six tractors into one trailer. They also found out that the cabs were not wanted on the tractors, so these were removed to save weight and space. After several trips, John approached Bob to ask if the drivers could collect the money from the agent after each delivery. Very sceptical about this idea, he decided to give it a try as John was an exceptionally good client, giving his word that the receiving customer's agent would pay up in whichever currency Bob requested. Sure enough, when the next

FULL LOADS — GROUPAGE

U.K. — EUROPE — SCANDINAVIA — ASIA — EIRE

TRANS UK CONTINENTAL LIMITED

PROFESSIONAL INTERNATIONAL TRANSPORT

Tel : Felixstowe 77455/8   Telex : 98658

CRANE FRUEHAUF BUILDINGS, DOOLEY AVENUE, FELIXSTOWE. IP11 8HE.

Your Ref.

Our Ref.

Date   28th April 76

Attention of

J.Tuffan Esq
Tracter Import Co
Melton.

Dear Sir,

      We can offer you for the transporting of
tractors from Melton as follows, until shipping date
1st June 1976.

4 tractor to Istanbul £1425

4 tractor to Izmit   £1500

6 tractor to Izmit   £1660 (incl. £100 commission)

For shipments from 1st June 1976 the following rates
will apply

4 tractor to Istanbul £1525

4 tractor to Izmit   £1625

6 tractor to Izmit   £1775 (incl £100 commission)

To be paid in full in DM at destination.
Rate of exchange as published in Finantial Times on
day of loading + 5%.

Shipment to be effected 3/4 working days from loading
unless notified in wring or telex.

TRANS UK CONTINENTAL   J.TUFFAN

Rate schedule for the tractor work to Turkey.

> *We were having quite a few issues with the Volvo F86s and F88s we were running to the Middle East.*

load was delivered to the customs compound on the Asian side of the Bosphorus, the driver drove back to the Mocamp, took a taxi down town, walked across the Galata Bridge to the agent's office and, while drinking a couple of sugary chais, waited for the cash to be counted out, usually in German Marks!

There was a huge amount of trust invested in this operation; firstly that the agent would stump up the cash, and secondly that the drivers could be relied on not to 'lose' it. It says a lot about Bob's respect for his employees and their mutual respect for him that no money ever went missing.

A proportion of this cash then formed the running money for the driver to get back to the UK and it also allowed for any extra cash to be passed on to any trucks heading down who might have run into mechanical difficulty. One of the unresolved problems of overland work had been the difficulty in obtaining emergency funds to deal with extraordinary situations. This cash on delivery development in some way helped to resolve this.

Bob mainly used his Volvo F86 trucks on this job, and would reload them with their regular bicycle contract from Yugoslavia for the UK.

"At the time", said Bob, "we were having quite a few issues with the Volvo F86s and F88s we were running to the Middle East. Even the 4,000-mile round trip to Istanbul was shaking them to bits, so rough was the road through Yugoslavia. The bracketry was constantly breaking or shaking bolts out, and it was taking a few days after every trip to get them repaired and ready to go again.

"In 1976, I was contacted by Peter Colby, who had by then taken on the franchise for Fiat Trucks. He asked me to come and look at some new tractor units that he'd recently had delivered.

Two Fiats in the depot at Sub-Station Road. Originally running on 'R' registration prefixes, the trucks were re-registered after a year as they were never taxed or used in the UK for their first twelve months.

Roy Gilbert's Fiat 619. This was the only trailer that Trans UK ran with its German agent's name on. Roy was engaged purely on German work for Trans UK.

Discharging a ro-ro ferry in Sharjah. Bob initially put the trailer on the ferry empty in Marseille, but when he was offered a load in Cyprus, he took the trailer off and loaded it up to double the pay!

German-registered Mercedes also loading tractors for Turkey.

Laden with Minis.

Paul Rowlands and Peter Ransome (left and right respectively) having a wrestle at Sibiu, Romania. Paul had been towed from Sebes by Steve Cooper when his water pump had failed. Four of them were en route to Tehran in the winter of 1975–6.

Paul Rowlands in West Germany. The trailer is the only one that Trans UK had with a red sheet. When the trailer was bought second-hand it had a new sheet on it so Bob decided he may as well just livery the red sheet instead of buying a new one. It was named Mi lady Jillie after John Scott's wife.

Terence Ludar Smith. Known to everyone as Smudger, he was the only Trans UK driver to deliver to Kuwait. Here he is having a cook up on the diesel tank.

"Being interested, as the Mitchell–Rowlands Fiat had been so successful, I went along, but sadly they were all day cabs. I told Peter they were no good to me as I had been to Tehran with Bob Crofton-Sleigh and seen what a nightmare it was for him in his day cab!

"He did give me a price though, and they were considerably cheaper than the equivalent new Volvos.

"A few days after I had been to see him, he called me to tell me he was having a number of day cabs converted into sleeper cabs, not by adding a small box on the back of the cab like Jennings were doing with Atkinson and the like, but by a company called LocoMotor in Andover doing a complete double sleeper conversion.

"A couple of weeks later I was invited up to have a look at the first ones that had been converted. They'd done such an impressive job I ended up buying all four of them!"

The Fiats spelt the end for Trans UK buying Volvos for the Middle East fleet; the Fiats were cheaper and mechanically more reliable, so they were an obvious choice.

Meanwhile, more and more 'Maggies' were added to the fleet, and even a 310 was purchased and sent to Tehran to evaluate its performance.

Numerous people were saying that they should not be sent that far as they were a bit of an unknown quantity in that environment

"Numerous people were saying that they should not be sent that far as they were a bit of an unknown quantity in that environment," said Bob, "but apart from a few minor faults the truck performed well. One major advantage was the fact that they were air-cooled rather than the 'conventional' water-cooled engines all the other truck manufacturers produced at the time. The turbocharged Volvos would often run hot in the Turkish mountains, but as the Maggies were air-cooled this was never a problem."

A lot of the Maggie 232s were on contract to Johnson Stevens Agencies, and were painted in its colours of brown, yellow and white in the same layout as the Trans UK paint job.

One problem that manifested itself fairly early on with the Maggies was that the brake adjustment was done differently to most trucks of the time. 'Smudger' Smith found out almost to his peril while on a trip to Tehran.

Delivering a full load of personal effects, he noticed that his brakes were not as effective as they should be, but with a low gross weight he wasn't too concerned. However, once he had tipped and reloaded with 17 tonnes of tank engines for the UK, the lack of efficient braking capacity rapidly raised its ugly head. With a 'proper' load on board, he soon found out that neither the unit nor trailer brakes were of any use! Nursing the truck as best as he could across the mountains of Turkey back into Europe and then all the way back to Zeebrugge docks to ship home proved to be a hair-raising experience.

Smudger takes up his story: "Driving the Maggie relatively cautiously through a Czechoslovakian village, as I was aware of the lorry's braking deficiencies, I watched as a child kicked a football out in front of me, and even though only doing 35mph it seemed to be about 100 yards before I could get the truck to stop, by which time I was covered in sweat from the shock of the experience. When I finally arrived back at Felixstowe docks, I got Bob to drive the truck back to the yard, and when we got there, he was as white as a sheet, and was stunned that I'd had managed to get the truck all the way back without a major mishap."

> *I got Bob to drive the truck back to the yard, and when we got there, he was as white as a sheet*

"I knew Smudger was good," said Bob, "but when the outfit was put on the brake tester, the only brake with any real effect was the offside front trailer wheel. I realized just how good a driver he was!"

Unlike the majority of truck manufacturers, the Magirus unit's brakes were actually adjusted in a different manner to the trailer, but no one actually knew this, so they were being adjusted in what was considered to be the 'normal' fashion. As the vehicle was on its first trip, Bob got a large refund off Parradines' dealership, as well as Eurofleet trailer rentals.

An oddball on the fleet was a one-off Scania 80, which was solely used for UK work. Bob purchased this from his brothers at W. Carter haulage after visiting their yard one day. They had bought it from Mann Farms at Bawdsey, but it was surplus to requirements, and as Bob was on the lookout for lightweight tractor units, he thought he would have a punt on it. He never had any intention of buying a Scania new, because he believed the much higher purchase price could not be justified. The little 80 proved itself to be a solid reliable truck that was just as good as any of the Volvo F86s in the fleet.

Another unintended oddball was an 'A' series ERF accrued as part of a larger purchase.

In 1978, Bob had bought out a local company, Page Bros., based at Capel St Mary, just south of Ipswich. It wanted to sell up and get out of transport. Several people were interested in buying the company, which included a yard and servicing facilities, but the Page family could not decide which one of them actually owned it!

Thanks to the fact that John Weedon was Bob's brother-in-law, as well as being Page's transport manager, Bob had a distinct advantage over the others who wanted to buy the business. On top of that, John had also been a subcontractor of Bob's for a period of time prior to calling it a day.

Unsure how to move forward with his intended purchase, Bob spoke to each member of the family about which part of the business they had decided to personally claim, yard/garage, etc., and offered each individual family member a price for their own piece to turn it into a job lot. Once he had an agreed price from everyone, he approached the bank about a loan to cover the purchases. Surprisingly, Bob's father, Leslie, stepped in, and offered to lend him the majority of the money for the purchase, with Bob making up the difference.

The sale went ahead with much of the vehicle ware being sold off to other hauliers. What was left was the one solitary ERF tractor unit, an odd trailer or two, and the yard and workshops, which became Trans UK's second depot.

One of Bob's drivers was a guy called Rupert Solomon, the son of a wealthy family who'd somehow got into transport and always fancied himself as a big time owner driver–subcontractor but had never gone out of his way to make the effort. However, one day, opportunity came knocking when an actual owner–driver turned up in the Felixstowe yard after making a delivery.

"He was at the end of his tether." remembers Bob, "He was so annoyed that he couldn't find a back load, and the truck wasn't paying, blah, blah, blah, that he'd had just about enough of everything, and was going to get rid of the truck as soon as he got back home!

"As it was an F86, I asked him how much he wanted for it. Within half an hour we'd done a deal, got his cheque written out and given him a lift to the train station!

"Rupert obviously thought this would be his big chance and, as he liked the look of the truck, offered me an acceptable price and had it painted in Trans UK colours to run as one of my subcontractors, paying me for it in instalments. Being a 'G' prefix, this truck should have had a chrome grille, but I had a black grille retro-fitted instead, to match the rest of the 86s in the fleet.

"One day I had a call from Norman, the fleet engineer at the Capel depot, asking why a trailer had come back covered in feathers! I knew what had happened straight away! Quite often the drivers on the Middle East run would pick up farmers and their chickens on the way back from Abadan up to Tehran for a bit of cash. Well if they are doing that I want a few notes as a thank you for using my truck! I guessed Steve Cooper had done this on the way back, so I gave him a call. He told me that he had put his hammock up in the trailer and his pillow had split, hence the feathers everywhere. I told him he best get down to Capel then with about ten empty pillow cases to fill them back up with all these feathers in the trailer!"

One particular job that didn't go to plan ended up as a major disaster and cost us a large amount of money.

"Of course, it wasn't all sunshine and sand," recalls Bob. "One particular job that didn't go to plan ended up as a major disaster and cost us a large amount of money.

"Occasionally when it was really busy I had to take on extra subcontractors that I didn't know as well as my regulars. The one who caused our company a huge amount of time and money was recommended by word of mouth, so I took him

COMMERCIAL MOTOR October 10 1975

TWO ...or the road

Two operators tell CM how they have beaten the 'bumps' out of the Middle East road

The Trans-UK book includes this photocopy of an Iran third-party insurance certificate so that the driver can verify the one that he has to buy on entry at the border.

What the Trans UK Continental driver's manual contains

Inside front cover: TIR Carnet

Page		Page	
1	Driver's authorisation from Trans UK.	2	Confirmation of extent of insurance.
3	Insurance cover notes and fuel credit card.	4	Carnet de passage for unit.
5	Carnet de passage for trailer.	6	GV60.
7	Mileage chart and basic transport law for Holland. Europort to German border.	8	Basic transit law Belgium.
9	Mileage chart for Belgium Zeebrugge to German border.	10	Basic law, West Germany, and vehicle identity certificate (completed at border).
11	Fuel check certificate for West Germany.	12	Mileage chart, West Germany. Aachen to Cologne and Aachen to Salzburg.
13	Information for vehicles travelling by German Federal Railways.	14	As page 13.
15	As page 13.	16	Copy of co-operation quota German permit.
17	German/Austrian passport control form and Austrian mileage charts.	18	Basic transport law, Austria.
19	Copy of Austrian permit.	20	Copy of Yugoslav permit.
21	Yugoslavian mileage chart.	22	Yugoslavian and Bulgarian basic transport laws.
23	Bulgarian mileage chart.	24	Turkish mileage chart.
25	Details of how to transit Turkey.	26	Turkish contacts for service and local Turkish law.
27	Explanatory notes on Turkish law.	28	As page 27.
29	As page 27.	30	A list of Turkish agents and the addresses of UK commercial representatives.
31	Mileage charts for Iran and agent's name and address.	32	Iranian insurance certificate and local transport law.
33	Detailed instructions on quantities and cost of fuel from Felixstowe to Tehran.	34	A fuel guide for the return journey.
35	General notes on conduct.	36	Conversion tables for weights and cash.
37	Conversion rates for cash and clothing sizes.	38	Maximum weights and dimensions of vehicles Europe.
39	As page 38.	40	International driving permit, vaccination and innoculation certificates and certificate of religion.
41	CMR note.	42	Goods manifest.
43	Instructions to drivers on points of contact with Felixstowe.	44	Reload instructions.

Inside back cover : European service manual. Driver's guide. Ty breakdown service manual. Fuel bunkering service in Europe. Mileage cha for Greece. Stamped addressed envelopes. Driver's passport.

ONLY a brave man or a fool would claim that he could accurately state the road transit time between the UK and any point beyond Bulgaria. The contingencies the driver has to meet in Europe, west or east, can normally be catered for; but beyond the Bulgarian border things are vastly different. It is from here on that delays occur and the profit margin on jobs disappears.

Many of the delays can be traced to bad driver briefing and this in turn can be attributed to inadequate reconnaissance and pre-planning by the operator.

Mr Robert Carter, managing director of Trans UK Continental Ltd, has compiled one of the most detailed driver's manuals in use on the trans-European Middle East run. He did not depend on secondhand information or the written advice issued by either the trade associations, consulates or the trade press, although he admits that all of this proved helpful in the initial stages.

Bob, the son of Leslie Carter, an East Anglian haulier, is experienced in all aspects of road haulage and holds an hgv1 licence. He also has inside knowledge of the operations of shipping and forwarding agencies. It therefore came easy to him to get behind the wheel of a 32-ton outfit and lead a five-vehicle convoy to Tehran.

The result is a driver's manual which contains as much information as it is necessary and possible to carry, right down to pre-stamped and addressed airmail envelopes with ready-typed letters advising the Felixstowe office of Trans UK that each border has been crossed. This documentary evidence is shown to the customer; which he accepts, whereas there is just no proof to the customer that the driver has used the more conventional method of having "phoned the office."

The manual contains 22 transparent folder-type "pages," thus displaying 44 pages of material. It is arranged in the order in which the run will be made, with a mileage chart showing distances and routes between the points of entry to and exit from each country. There is detailed information on each country's traffic laws and border procedures and in addition to the originals of the permits the folder carries photostat copies.

As an example of the detail, in the Turkish section the drivers are advised that no matter how unreasonable the Turkish police might be there is no point in arguing with them "as they only delay the

Commercial Motor magazine ran a short piece on Bob's fabled 'Drivers bible', which Bob person prepared shadowing the first Middle Eastern trip. Photo: Commercial Motor

on in good faith. He was a Scotsman by the name of Jim McClusky, who was running a couple of vehicles out of Diss, in Norfolk. I offered him two loads, one was tractors to Istanbul, and one that already sat on rental trailers in our yard awaiting delivery to Tabriz in Northern Iran.

"Driving a Volvo F88, Jim McClusky was given the step frame trailer and his driver, James Campbell in an F86, a standard tilt trailer. Due to Bob's policy of no F86 going further than Turkey, James was to do the Istanbul, with Jim heading for Iran.

"Being Middle East 'virgins', so to speak, they were paired up with Paul Rowlands, who was already an experienced overland driver, and Freddie Grimble, to 'look after them'.

"This was standard procedure with Trans UK. After the inaugural trip in 1975 no inexperienced first tripper was expected to make the journey on his own.

"Shipping out from Felixstowe on 25th January 1976, the whole catastrophic trip finally came to an end on 7th July in the same year. It was a litany of mechanical and self-inflicted disasters and cost our company a huge amount of money. Paul soon realized that this would not be a simple straightforward 'babysitting' job and the four trucks took a week longer to get as far as Istanbul due to Jim's lack of interest in motivating himself to get up in the mornings!

"By the morning of the fourth day, *still* in Czechoslovakia, things had come to a head. James Campbell, a long-time friend and work colleague of Jim McClusky, had tried to rouse him for a 5am start and Paul went with him. When JC opened the unlocked door all Paul could hear was the sound of heavy snoring from the depths of the stale-smelling cab. When Paul lost his temper JC apologized profusely and explained that his boss was asleep!"

It was as if the machine was bouncing across the table in anger, I watched as the words spilled across the paper.

Eventually the mismatched band got to the Mocamp in Istanbul, where Paul immediately telexed Tony Waugh and explained the situation.

"Within twenty seconds the telex was rattling away in response," explained Paul. "It was as if the machine was bouncing across the table in anger, I watched as the words spilled across the paper. 'Leave the bloody idiots there, you can't afford to lose any more time and jeopardize future loads, they're subbies, they'll have to look after themselves Paul. Get going first thing in the morning, All the best. Tony.' Ultimately that turned out to be a good decision!"

Bob takes up the tale, recounting as much as he knows and information gleaned from some of the original telexes he still retains.

"On the 21st of February, already three weeks overdue, Jim managed to leave Istanbul and got as far as Adapazari, before we received a telex saying that a wheel bearing had collapsed on his trailer and could we send out 200 quid with his son,

Tom, to cover some expenses! The wheel bearing wasn't too much of a drama, as such were the horrendous road conditions back then it was a regular occurrence to have some sort of breakdown. He either managed to fix it himself or get one of the local Turkish 'metal magicians' to do a running repair on it.

"No sooner had that problem been cured than he was telexing us again telling us that his truck's differential had packed up! He had though, managed to make some progress and had now reached Ankara. The only thing we could do to assist with his diff problem was to send a spare down in a Land Rover with Cotton Trucking, who was already taking a turbo to Kapicule for 'Smudger' Smith! Hopefully the diff should arrive with him in ten days or so."

In the meantime, James Campbell was still manfully plugging away, round tripping Turkey for Trans UK to hopefully help offset the costs that were slowly building up.

"As far as I remember," recounts Bob, "James managed to complete at least three trips to Istanbul before we received a telex from him on 21st April stating that he was in Jihlava, Czechoslovakia, with a broken clutch and could we organize getting him towed to Brno and help finance a repair.

> *Eventually, out of the blue, we heard that Jim McClusky had actually reached Erzurum*

"Meanwhile, we'd heard nothing from Jim McClusky other than Cotton Trucking reporting back on his return that they'd managed to effect a repair to his diff and he was at last mobile again!

"Eventually, out of the blue, we heard that Jim McClusky had actually reached Erzurum about 20th April and things had gone from bad to worse!

"Apparently he'd parked somewhere that had showers, I was told a hotel, somewhere on the outskirts of Erzurum, about 300 miles from the Iranian border, and on parking up decided to have a few drinks, which was quite normal for many of the drivers on this type of work. The act of parking up for a beer was normally called 'Efes Kontrol' by truckers, named after Efes, the only potable beer in Turkey.

Unfortunately, the amount he had to drink overcame his ability to stand up properly, and while still drunk he fell over in the shower, smashing his head badly on the porcelain and ending up being hospitalized. Along with this information came further requests for cash to pay vehicle repair and hospital bills to the tune of 15000TL (£500).

"We then started receiving telexes from a Turkish agent, Turtrans, a company that we'd had no dealings with before, saying, could we please submit monies to them owed by 'our employee', Mr Jim McClusky, and a figure of 9550TL (£280) for assistance given to him!

"Unbeknown to us back at the office, while in hospital, he'd lent his tractor unit to another owner–driver who was having vehicle problems of his own, allowing his new 'friend' to carry on with *his* job to Tehran. This took yet *another* fortnight while he waited for his truck to return.

"By now he was months behind schedule, and we hadn't really heard from him other than his continuous requests for assistance and cash. The decision was made to fly James Campbell out to Turkey to take over the truck and at least try and get the damn trailer unloaded!

"When James arrived, Jim simply refused to give him control of the truck and instead rode shotgun with him to the Iranian border.

"Being as procedures are somewhat different out there, he had to walk through the border as a regular tourist, and he managed to hitch a ride to our agent, Deugro, in Tehran. He sent us a telex on 5th June, four months after leaving the UK! Normally a trip to Tehran takes two weeks on average! James was by now totally fed up with Jim, and frankly we were as well. Finally, Jim managed to get it down to Tehran, clear customs and get unloaded, while James flew back to the UK to set off with another load of tractors for Istanbul in his own truck.

"While heading back towards Europe, Jim ran into the back of another truck, doing a fair bit of damage to his cab, but not enough to put it off the road thankfully, and he managed to limp his way back as far as Istanbul Mocamp.

While heading back towards Europe, Jim ran into the back of another truck, doing a fair bit of damage to his cab

"It was now the start of July and McClusky had taken six months to date!

"By the time he got there, James had already arrived at the Mocamp, and was having a day off before putting his paperwork in for the delivery. He was having a sunbathe in the truck park, and naturally as the sun goes round in the day, he kept moving himself around to follow it. Unfortunately, some time in the afternoon, he moved a bit too far and a taxi ran over his legs! This was the final straw for me. It was now the 7th of July, and I just wanted an end to this sad saga. I decided to get Jim's truck loaded into the back of his step frame, and he could sleep inside it. I had two trucks delivering in Istanbul at the time, so Peter Ransome and 'Smudger' Smith were called upon to help. We really had to get the trailer back as it was a rental and was costing us a fortune. Smudger's trailer was stripped down to make a flatbed and loaded with Peter's empty trailer. Peter pulled the step frame back to West Germany, and Smudger took their own 'topped' up trailers back to their agents, where they could unload the trailers, load them for the UK and get everyone home at long last."

The Pakistan work, as well as the Afghanistan work, all came about in 1977 through one man in London, who was probably the only customer that Bob didn't meet personally. He owned what used to be called a 'bucket shop', which sold last-minute airline tickets and the like. He was buying lots of new and second-hand white goods, which were for export.

"I am guessing that he saw one of our trucks in London one day and thought he would give us a call and see if we could help him out," Bob recalls. "The paperwork was enormous for the loads. Every single item on the manifest, from a kettle to a cooker, had to have its own separate papers. This didn't bother us as no matter how many items there were on the trailer, it always went to the same place in Lahore where everything would be unloaded. At the time the law was that every single Pakistani citizen was allowed the importation of one or two items of white goods per year."

Driver Michael 'Micky' Prigg was a regular driver on this service, and thrived on it. Armed with a cheeky grin and happy-go-lucky attitude, nothing was too much of a problem.

> *Armed with a cheeky grin and happy-go-lucky attitude, nothing was too much of a problem.*

Once, while driving at night through the Khyber Pass (night driving was something Bob had generally warned against once out of Europe), Mick came across a small pick-up truck, which was in a ditch. Without even thinking he stopped to help the three men get their pick-up out of the ditch. They were all extremely grateful, and insisted that Mick should follow them. As they were driving along, Mick could hear various whistles coming from the pick-up in front, but didn't think too much of it. They took him to a safe area at the end of the pass for him to park up for the night and bade him farewell. He later found out that the whistles were to their other friends hiding in the mountains waiting to ambush vehicles, but due to him stopping and helping he was allowed a safe passage through!

Trans UK didn't do a lot of Afghan deliveries, as the trucks were generally full for Pakistan, it was somewhere to reload from after delivering to Pakistan, usually from their agents, Afghan International Transport. Carpets or animal hides were generally the return loads from Afghanistan. International Moving Services Pakistan was the Pakistani agent, which would arrange any reloads if it had anything when the trucks were empty, but if anything was not ready within a day or so from either agent, the trucks would come back empty to Europe because the bicycle traffic back from Yugoslavia was so busy they could only just keep up with their demand for trucks.

Getting across to Lahore in Pakistan involved crossing the Attock Bridge. As with a lot of passes and bridges, it had developed slowly and had certainly not kept pace with modern life and development. Getting into and also out from the bridge involved a 90 degree turn; not so much of a problem in a car or a small van, but incredibly tight for an articulated truck and trailer. In fact, one of Bob's trucks got jammed against the side while trying to enter the bridge once, and was stuck for almost twelve hours. Therefore no traffic flowed either way for half of the day! The bridge had a soldier posted at either end to assist in directions for the trucks to

Mick Prigg. A regular on the Afghanistan run, talented engineer and mechanic, and always armed with a joke up his sleeve. Here he is sporting the local 'attire' in Afghanistan.

Mick Prigg grabbing a quick forty winks.

In the mountains. Photo: Mick Prigg

Queuing at Bazargan. Photo: Mick Prigg

Kicking up the dust in Turkey. Photo: Mick Prigg

Eastern Turkey. Photo: Mick Prigg

Empty and heading west again to reload.

Pulling a Davis Turner trailer on the regular run to Piraeus docks.

Malcolm Howe relaxing in his truck at the border. Photo: Gerry Keating

Tim Smith with his Fiat at Afghanistan customs. Photo: Gerry Keating

Gerry photographed by Malcolm Howe. The pair were stuck at the Afghanistan–Pakistan border for three weeks due to paperwork problems. Note the bulge in Malcolm's trailer where the load has moved. Photo: Gerry Keating

Repairing a tyre in Pakistan. Photo: Gerry Keating

Mick Prigg in Pakistan with Tim Smith's broken down Fiat, which was suffering from problems with its batteries.

**Gerry's Fiat and an
Afghan International
trailer in their yard
in Kabul. Photo:
Gerry Keating**

enter the bridge, but it soon became apparent to the drivers that the best thing to do was to completely ignore them and judge it for yourself!

Gerry Keating, another regular on this work, also had quite an eventful trip, as he recounts: "I got home from one trip to find out that Bob had a truck that had broken down in Afghanistan, so I volunteered to fly out and retrieve it. The gearbox had broken and Fiat were flying one out for fitment. He wouldn't have any of it as I had just got home, and I was told to have my time off and not to worry about it. Well I had my time off, and when I came back to work Bob asked me to fly out to Pakistan to then make my way to the border where the truck was, to start making my way back with it."

The truck had been left at Trans UK's agent Afghan International's transport yard, which had repaired the stricken truck. Gerry then drove to a regular parking area in Kabul called Hotel Goulza, which was a hotel with a secure compound parking area within the customs compound. The Ayatollah Ruhollah Khomeini had gained power in Iran, and there was no chance of getting in to go back home. No foreigners were allowed in, so the only way back would be on a ferry. He was going to have to take the truck into Pakistan and then south to Karachi to put the truck on a ferry that would eventually go to England.

I got home from one trip to find out that Bob had a truck that had broken down in Afghanistan, so I volunteered to fly out and retrieve it.

It took two weeks of constant journeys to and from customs agents and the various embassies before he could get under way. The window of opportunity to deal with all these people was only three days in a week. The Pakistani weekend is Thursday and Friday and the British embassy was shut on Saturdays and Sundays, leaving Monday to Wednesday.

The first problem he had was that on arrival back at the border the load was not allowed through. It had been loaded with animal hides, but with them sitting in a trailer for that long they had gone 'off', so to speak. So they had to be returned to where they were loaded from first. Then a reload was found for the truck from the British embassy in Lahore, Pakistan. So this was loaded on to the truck, and he was ready to go again. He was then told he would have to go to the border at Torkham to clear customs before heading for Karachi. So he went back to the border again. Then the next problem arose. Despite the fact that all the goods were for export, someone in authority decided that it was internal haulage, and that a UK-registered truck was not allowed to undertake such a journey! So it was back to Lahore yet again. The truck was unloaded again, and this time all the goods were put on to a train. The train went down to Karachi port, and Gerry followed the train down there in the empty truck, where it was all reloaded on to the truck, and he finally drove on to the ferry! Gerry sailed with the truck as far as Mumbai in India, where he decided to fly home instead of spending the next few weeks at sea on a freight boat.

Gerry's truck with one from Trans UK's agents, Afghan International, in Afghan's yard in Kabul. Photo: Gerry Keating

Tim Smith meditating in front of his stricken Fiat.

Gerry Keating en route home after a long trip to Pakistan. Photo: Gerry Keating

Moving around at a border waiting to get papers done, which could take anywhere from two to five days. No toilets, no shops, huts with officials who work 8am – 4pm, with lunch 12pm – 2pm, shut Fridays and Saturdays. Photo: Gerry Keating

At Torkham border, a Swiss-registered Volvo awaits clearance. Photo: Gerry Keating

Torkham border crossing after the Ayatollah had taken over Iran. He was the only thing on the road between Kabul and Karachi. Photo: Gerry Keating

Torkham border.

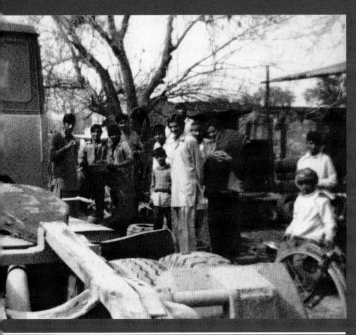

Gerry had to drop his trailer at the border and take his tractor unit through the Khyber Pass with a trailer tyre that needed repairing. The first village he came to had the facilities to fix it. Photo: Gerry Keating

Gerry and Malcolm seen heading for Pakistan, 1978. Photo: Gerry Keating

Back in England from Afghanistan. Although the photo quality is not that great, you can see that Malcolm, whose Fiat is the right-hand one, has been following Gerry, as his truck is filthy! Photo: Gerry Keating

Mar. 5   Down-Town Karachi
                          Parked on the street.
                          Temp. in shade 95° F.
                          Temp in the cab 100 +++

                          Surrounded by dust, dirt
flies, touts, beggars etc etc

Dear Pat & Family,
                                    How are you
all?   Well I hope and working
hard.   I forget when I sent my last
card or letter - Kabul?   It took
2 weeks there of daily visits to
customs & various ministries to
get the truck released and signed on
& my passport.   They only work
from   9.30 - 3.30   except lunch
break   &   not on Thurs or Fri
(Moslem w/e)   and   B. Embassy doesn't

Gerry's letter home from the border. Photo: Gerry Keating

102

Make/Model	Configuration	Reg	Name
Fiat	4x2 rigid flatbed	EEX 738T	Sherberton Gay Gordon
Fiat Florino	van	KPV 582V	Dartmoor's Dinkum
Fiat 130	4x2	VPU 973S	Cawsand Huckleberry
Fiat 130	4x2	DLH 597T	Sherberton Two Step
Fiat 130	4x2	EEX 733T	Manaton Bowerman
Fiat 170	4x2	EEX 734T	Midgehope Sorrel
Fiat 170	4x2	EEX 735T	Cosden Tomboy
Fiat 170	4x2	ELR 651T	Cawsand Boy
Fiat 170	4x2	SCL 871R re-registered WVG 305S	Dartmoor's Dinkum
Fiat 170	4x2	VCL 382S	Cawsand Hail
Fiat 170	4x2	VOY 456S	Dartmoor's Brightling
Fiat 170	4x2	VOY 461S	Dartmoor's Yeo
Fiat 170	4x2	VOY 474S	Yeoland Lord Nelson
Fiat 170	4x2	DLH 589T	Sherberton Extra Dry
Fiat 619	4x2	OCL 191P	Sherberton Newman
Fiat 619	4x2	OCL 192P	Dartmoor's Sparkling
Fiat 619	4x2	REX 604R, re-registered WVG 308S	Cawsand Romeo
Fiat 619	4x2	REX 605R re-registered WVG 311S	Cawsand Caliph
Fiat 619	4x2	REX 606R re-registered WVG 306S	Hele Prince
Fiat 619	4x2	REX 607R re-registered WVG 307S	Cawsand Boy
Fiat 619	4x2	RNG 110R	Hele Hussar
Magirus Deutz 232	van	CHK 957T	Manaton Punchinello
Magirus Deutz 232	4x2	EVW 70T	Cosden Major
Magirus Deutz 232	4x2	EVW 72T	Dartmoor's Redwing
Magirus Deutz 232	4x2	JWC 692V	Cawsand Romeo
Magirus Deutz 232	4x2 Day cab	TMB 873R	unknown
Magirus Deutz 232	4x2 Day cab	RWC 192M	unknown
Magirus Deutz 232	4x2	XRT 865S	Walreddon Musketeer
Magirus Deutz 232	4x2	XRT 866S	Cawsand Cavalier
Magirus Deutz 232	4x2	NPU 659P	Cosden Major
Magirus Deutz 232	4x2	NKO 848P	Hele Lancer
Magirus Deutz 232	4x2	RKJ 60R	Dunnabridge Bonny Boy
Magirus Deutz 232	4x2	LLV 205R	Manaton Nutcracker
Magirus Deutz 232	4x2	TVX 247R	Manaton Punchinello
Magirus Deutz 232	4x2	UGF 253R	Manaton Heather King
Magirus Deutz 232	4x2	XOO 123S	Cawsand Black Velvet
Magirus Deutz 310	4x2	GLC 537N	Cawsand Dancer
Magirus Deutz 310	4x2	LTG 474P	Moortown Prince Charming
Magirus Deutz 310	4x2	PAL 525R	Dartmoor's Redwing
Magirus Deutz 310	4x2	KHJ 956V	Hele Prince
Volvo F86	4x2	EPV 642L	Cosden Major
Volvo F86	4x2	PBJ 849M	Walreddon Musketeer
Volvo F86	4x2	SBJ 152M	Cawsand Cavalier
Volvo F86	4x2	SRT 906M	Hele Lancer
Volvo F86	4x2	WRT 419M	Dunnabridge Bonny Boy
Volvo F86	4x2	GBJ 620N	Hillenvale Goshawk
Volvo F86	4x2	PDD 416G	Rupert the Bear
Volvo F88	4x2	ELU 922J	Pennwood Forge Mill
Volvo F88	4x2	XTW 684L	Stroller- renamed Dartmoor's Childe
Volvo F88	4x2	GPW 355N	Cawsand Black Velvet
Volvo F88	4x2	GPW 356N	Ray Barrow Pool
Volvo F88	4x2	LNG 825P	Hele Brownie
Ford Transit	van	PMP 32R	Dartmoor's Yeo
Ford Transit	van	LRT 420K	Little Keg
Ford Transit	flatbed van	KRT 529P	unnamed
MAN 16.232	4x2	GMG 26N	Dartmoor's Brightling
MAN 16.232	4x2	SUV 719N	Dunnabridge Redstart
ERF A series	4x2	GBJ 317J	Robert Emmet
Scania 81	4x2	TEV 816N	Sherberton Newman
Atkinson Leader	6x2	YBJ 149G	Dartmoor's Childe

Trans UK Fleet List

March 1979

Down town Karachi, parked on the street.
Temperature in the shade, 95 degrees Fahrenheit, temperature in the cab 100+
Surrounded by dust, dirt, flies, touts, beggars etc.

Dear Pat and family

How are you? Well I hope and working hard. I forget when I sent my last card and letter, Kabul?

It took two weeks there of daily visits to customs and various ministries to get the truck released and signed onto my passport. They only work from nine thirty to three thirty, except for lunch break, and not on Thursday or Friday (Muslim weekends), and the British embassy doesn't work Saturday or Sunday either. So all in all, I did well to get the truck so quickly.

I was out and down the Kabul gorge about three to four days before the fighting started there again. I then took one week in Lahore customs, before getting rid of the load of skins, and getting a reload. However, once reloaded, they then said I couldn't transit Pakistan to Karachi, but had to return to Afghanistan and transit from north to south of the whole country in one go. Of course, once I got to the north border, customs there said I couldn't transit north to south, but had to return to Lahore! So, back to Lahore, and unloaded in the customs area and transfer the goods into railway trucks to be railed to Karachi while I came down empty.

The trip down was hell. Thousand and ninety-six kilometres of single track, potholes, dirt, rocks, bumpy roads, where top speed varied between 5 and 25mph. The only one good section stretch of ninety-eight miles from Hyderabad to Karachi, where there is a toll road, equivalent of a B road in England. The heat and flies and mosquitos at night are not pleasant. But I haven't been ill on this trip yet, touch wood! I've been here a week now waiting to get the good reloaded on the truck, and customs clearance. But, are they slow, and lazy, and dirty! There are a couple of streams of open sewers through the city, and masses of filth and dirt every-where. The heat of course makes it worse.

I'm hoping to get the truck on a ship, Ro-Ro service to Felixstowe on the fourteenth of March. If its not loaded and customs cleared, the next one is about a month later. I am sup-posed to fly back when I have seen the truck safely on the ship, but I am now short of money. I had the extra expenses of Lahore to Afghanistan border and return. Also a broken trailer frame to get welded and straightened as well as the daily drain of taxis to agents, customs, shippers and many days living, so I shall try to get a passage back on a boat. The Ro-Ro boat is non-passenger.

Well, au revoir and keep well

Gerry

Gerry's letter. (He was flown out to retrieve a truck, which the driver had left out there and had flown home.)

Mick Prigg got stopped at Peshawar, (the entry city after the Khyber Pass into Pakistan) on one trip, which was highly unusual. Unbeknown to Trans UK, the whole Pakistan operation had been a big fiddle! The Pakistani authorities had found out what had been going on, so Mick was detained at the border for several days. In the end they commandeered a shed and unloaded the truck completely, signed off his paperwork and gave him an exit stamp for Afghanistan.

"We eventually found out that each individual weigh bill for the loads had fictional consignees that the man in London had created. But we had been paid for the delivery so we were not out of pocket! It was a shame it ended as the drivers enjoyed the route, and the rate Trans UK was getting was also pretty good," Bob remembers.

It wasn't just the Middle East work that was booming. Trans UK also had a truck departing every day to Mulheim in West Germany for its agent, Gunter Baumann. This often worked out well as it was then able to offer another excellent customer, Claas agricultural machinery at Saxham, near Bury St Edmunds, a guaranteed twenty-four hour express delivery service back from West Germany. Whenever a truck arrived at the Claas factory at Harswinkel, anything that was there to go, went, whether it was one pallet of spares or a full trailer load. Trans UK was also involved in the logistics of getting combine harvesters and other large machinery to Claas' depot once they arrived via ferry in Felixstowe.

One evening, Bob was in a muddle. His driver, Ray Rainham, was due to ship out with a load of tractors for Istanbul, but his wife had got so fed up with him being away she had taken his passport and threatened to set fire to it.

'Taffy' had shipped into Felixstowe that morning, and upon hearing this story and the problem Bob had, he decided he would ship straight back out. He borrowed the office telephone, put his handkerchief over the receiver and called his wife. He told her that he had been badly delayed in Romania on his way home, and that he wouldn't get back for another couple of weeks. He then went straight to the supermarket for some fresh supplies, and was back on the same boat that he shipped into Felixstowe on in the morning!

As the UK side of the business expanded to meet demand, more and more vehicles were added to the fleet

As the UK side of the business expanded to meet demand, more and more vehicles were added to the fleet, some of which were painted up in customer's liveries, such as the two Magirus Deutz that were bought and dedicated to 'C. Shaw Lovell'.

One contract entailed delivering two containers daily, at 8am and 2pm, to DuPont's factory at Alfreton, near Derby. There the drivers simply dropped a trailer with a loaded container and returned with an empty one to the docks.

Further divisions in the company were also created, Trans UK Forwarding and Trans UK Holdings. The Forwarding part was to deal with customs clearance, for themselves and third parties. Phillip Greenfield and John Scott were assigned as managers of this part of the company.

Meanwhile, Bob had spotted the company 'logo', 'you call, we haul', was being used by another haulier on the front of its vehicles. To counteract this, You Call We Haul Ltd was registered at Companies House, thereby preventing anyone else using it.

"The name was part of our company identity, a type of slogan. We used to get potential clients phoning up and when we answered they would say, 'is that You Call, We Haul?' So I knew the benefit of having it liveried on our trucks."

> *We used to get potential clients phoning up and when we answered they would say, is 'that You Call, We Haul?'*

One day in 1976, while passing Frankfurt, Steve Cooper's Volvo F88 developed a worryingly loud knocking noise. Managing to find a phonebox at Medenbach and contact the office, Bob was able to diagnose the problem over the phone. He concluded that the main end bearing was on its way out, and that the truck would need towing back for repair.

Arrangements were made for the trailer to be dropped and for one of the trucks doing the daily groupage run to collect it and bring it back to Baumann's depot. In the meantime, Bob set off in his Range Rover to recover the tractor unit and on arrival simply attached the unit to his Range Rover with a straight bar and proceeded to tow it back to Zeebrugge for shipping to Felixstowe! What a sight that must have been going down the motorway. Now and again they had to stop for Steve to run the engine and allow the unit to build up sufficient air for the brakes to work.

"Bugger", said Bob, as within 20 miles of the border at Aachen, the German motorway police pulled them over and unsurprisingly declared that this was totally illegal in Germany! A recovery truck was ordered to drag the stricken Volvo to the Belgium border at Aachen and drop it off, where, out of sight of the Belgian Police, Bob promptly hooked back up and managed to get it all the way to Zeebrugge for shipping home.

"It was a bit scary at times," Bob recalls. "As long as the truck had air in the system Steve could help me with the braking, but if he didn't see what I had seen or didn't have enough air it was just me trying to stop the whole lot. As you can imagine, the thing just pushed me along! We had a few scary moments and close shaves, but it all worked out well in the end."

Obviously, with a growing fleet there were always going to be an occasional roadside breakdown, some of which the driver could repair, some a local garage and some Bob went out to repair himself. Another such 'continental' trip Bob went to rectify at the roadside was when 'Smudger' Smith's Volvo F86 developed a suspected head gasket problem. He had got as far as the German–Czechoslovakian border at Weidhaus, so Bob loaded up the Humber Sceptre with all the spares he

1981, the end of the road. The yard shortly before the final sale of all the equipment. The Magirus in the foreground has been painted red, but no one seems to remember why this was. It was last seen by Smudger Smith on a subsequent trip to Arabia abandoned in the desert in Saudi Arabia.

Waiting for the auctioneer's hammer.

Left over from when Bob bought out Page Brothers transport, the sole ERF in the Trans UK fleet was only used locally.

The last truck that Bob bought when running Trans UK. Uniquely, this was the only Fiat the company owned that had a Fuller gearbox fitted.

might need; spare heads, radiators, hoses, etc., and with one of Duffields' fitters too, met Smudger in a layby just outside Czechoslovakian customs. The head gasket was changed successfully and each went on their way. On returning to Dover, Bob was queuing in the lanes back ready to go through the customs shed when a customs officer walked past and asked what was in the car (due to the back end almost scraping the road!) Bob replied: "You don't want to know, although it won't bother customs!"

Well, of course, this piqued the man's interest and Bob had to show him all the spare parts, and explain what they had just been and done. The official was quite impressed and decided that, as he'd already seen the stuff, if Bob went into customs shed and had to do all this again this would delay everyone else. So he radioed to one of his colleagues on a side gate, and he sneaked Bob straight out of the docks and on to the A2!

> *You don't want to know, although it won't bother customs!*

Bob also had a rather infuriating breakdown to attend to in Yugoslavia. John 'Taffy' Dinwiddy had phoned in and said that he couldn't build any air up

News Release

Press Officer: ANTHONY SMITH

FIAT

Fiat Commercial Vehicles Ltd
Reg. No. 1239252 England

24 Concord Road, London W3
Tel: 01-992 5321
Telex: 932334

Felixstowe haulier Robert Carter of Trans-UK Ltd. has added three

FIAT 130 NT tractor units to his fleet to bring the total to 39

vehicles. With 20 FIATs in the fleet, the majority of which are

619T and 170NT26 units, Mr. Carter needed lightweight vehicles to

haul the lighter 20ft   30ft containers. The possibility of 16 ton

vehicles was considered, but these could only be re-loaded once they

had returned to base, while articulated trailers could be pre-loaded

to be collected on the return of the units. In addition a 16 ton

vehicle would only have allowed a 10 ton payload while the FIAT 130NT

when combined with the correct trailer can haul up to 50% more than a 16

ton vehicle, i.e. 15 tons. The vehicles were supplied by Peter Colby

Commercials Ltd. of Wymondham, Norfolk.

IVECO

Press release for an order of three new lightweight Fiat tractor units.

You Call

PROFESSIONAL INTERNATIONAL TRANSPORT

TRANS UK CONTINENTAL LIMITED

We Haul

NEW TRAILERS — NEW TRUCKS, ADD UP
TO AN EVEN BETTER SERVICE.
SPECIALISTS IN TRANSPORTATION TO
THE MIDDLE EAST.

Also 12 metre TIR tilt and box trailers available daily for all
E.E.C., Balkan, Scandinavian, Greek and Turkish
destinations. Bi-weekly, driver accompanied, groupage
services from main towns throughout the UK to the
Netherlands, Belgium and West Germany. Complete
shipping, forwarding, and customs documentation
services.

FULL U.K. TRANSPORTATION FACILITIES AVAILABLE
For professional transportation abroad (and in U.K.) contact:

TRANS U.K. CONTINENTAL LTD.

DOCK ROAD, FELIXSTOWE. TEL. 77455/8 TELEX 98658 ENGLAND

You call we haul. Bob's slogan, which was often used by other hauliers.

in the truck and trailer to get moving. Bob loaded up his car with spares for any eventuality, and took his yardman, Tommo, to help with the driving. It didn't take long in mainland Europe for Bob to realize that Tommo would not do any driving due to it being on the other side of the road to England. Stopping only for coffee and to use the toilets, they drove non-stop down to the Yugoslavian border. Due to it being communist, they would not be allowed to import spare parts to the country, and so they posed as tourists and used the tourist part of the border for cars, bluffing their way through. They eventually found Taffy just north of the town of Nis, parked outside a shady looking café. Within minutes, Bob had diagnosed a broken pipe to the range change on the gearbox, a quick and simple fix! He took the broken pipe into Nis itself, and managed to find a depot belonging to the Yugoslavian national transport company. Despite a complete language barrier, he managed to get himself understood by the mechanics at the depot, and get a repair to the pipe. They point black refused to take any money for the repair, and so Bob left them a carton of cigarettes as a thank you. Getting swiftly back to Taffy, and getting the truck repaired, Bob turned for home. Coming back through Austria, he persuaded Tommo to do some driving so he could try and get some sleep. This didn't even last for one hour as he was not used to being on the right-hand side, and kept drifting across the central line, and so Bob had to take over again. He managed to make it as far as Germany, and decided enough was enough. Driving any further would simply be too dangerous, it was time for a sleep. After all, they could catch the next ferry back to Felixstowe.

Within minutes, Bob had diagnosed a broken pipe to the range change on the gearbox, a quick and simple fix!

Working for a company called Wacro Lines, Bob rented trailers that were shipped unaccompanied to Lagos, Nigeria. These were mostly flatbed trailers, either rented ones or Trans UK's own. After a few round trips of the trailers, it became apparent that any good tyres that went out fitted to them would never be seen again, and so they had to make sure that only tyres that would be deemed illegal on UK roads were fitted when they were loaded on to the ship in Felixstowe. Bob also went on to supply a Volvo F86 to go out to unload and load the ships, due to a lack of any sort of dock shunter in Lagos. The truck was the same one that he had got back off Rupert Solomon after selling it to him a few years earlier. Eventually this truck was also shipped back into the UK at the end of the contract, although it was in no fit state to go back on the road due to the abuse and harshness of the docks in Lagos.

The transportation of alcohol also provided a steady stream of work for Trans UK, all within the UK. French wine was hauled to Coleman's of Norwich in trailers that had been sent over unaccompanied for a French haulier. Upon the return of one trailer to the yard after successfully delivering in Norwich, Tommo just happened to turn one of the taps on the tank trailer, and about a gallon of wine spilled

JOHN PARRADINE AND MAGIRUS DEUTZ EXPAND TOGETHER

Life on the open road behind the wheel of his own truck looked very attractive to John Parradine after years spent as a Japanese prisoner of war working on the Burma railway. The mere fact that he and his wife Ruth had to sell almost all their wordly possessions to buy that first second-hand Bedford was not enough to deter him. The young couple moved into a room of his brother's farm house and began to build up a transport business that has prospered for over 30 years. R. C. Parradine, who was known affectionately as John by friends and customers alike, was a first class mechanic and, until his sudden death in February 1978, he continued to take charge of the workshop side of the haulage and truck sales business he and his son were then running between them.

The younger John Parradine speaks with respect and affection of the father who built up the business by making the most of his opportunities. When his father first began in haulage he was carting a load of straw to London for £2.50, making good time back in order to take a second load the same night. He began to turn the tide in his financial affairs when the war surplus army sales got under way in the early fifties. He would buy job lots of ex-army trucks and jeeps. Those that could be repaired he worked on to sell at a reasonable profit, others that were beyond redemption were stripped down and cannabilised. The wheels and axles were often the only parts that were readily any good and it upset John Parradine to think of them going to waste. They did not for long because he soon realised he could convert them into farm trailers for which there was a ready market around his home village of Great Easton, near Dunmow. All the time he was dealing in these former military vehicles John Parradine was also building up his haulage business so that, by the time the sales came to an end, he was able to concentrate on this aspect of his operation.

From being an owner driver John Parradine Ltd. gradually expanded to its current operating strength of ten tractor units with plans for even further expansion under the progressive chairmanship of John Parradine junior. His mother, Ruth, is still a working director of the company she helped form with her husband and John's wife, Sara, is director of the sister company Essex Truck Sales Ltd. Parradine Haulage are involved in a considerable amount of container and tilt work out of Harwich and Felixstowe, and during the Winter months they are still called upon to handle a large volume of sugar beet from local farms. The expansion of the business created a need for a modern office block on their Great Easton depot about four years ago, and it was also at about that time that John Parradine Ltd. first became involved with Magirus Deutz. We ran that first truck and were really surprised and pleased with its performance, but there was no local agent to supply the vehicles or spares."

Within a year he and his father had persuaded Magirus to grant them an agency to sell their trucks under the name Essex Truck Sales Ltd. They had already realised it was no good offering to sell the vehicles without being able to provide a full back up service. To ensure that any new customers for Magirus Deutz vehicles would not experience the same problems over spares and servicing that they had encountered they set up a workshop with a full parts department. Today, in addition to their fully equipped workshop at Great Easton, they have equipped a three ton Magirus as a mobile stores and another similar vehicle as

a mobile workshop to do on site servicing and repairs to give their customers an even better service. Next year there are plans for an even larger and more modern workshop to be built at their depot to cope with the expansion of their truck sales division and subsequent servicing requirements of their customers.

With an investment of £100,000 in spares stocked at Great Easton, John Parradine feels justified in saying they can normally supply anything required from stock, but should a part be out of stock it can normally be obtained within 24 hours through their close links with Magirus Deutz Great Britain Ltd. in Cheshire. "Spares availability is one of the major selling points with any truck today," explains John Parradine, "haulage operators need to keep down time to the absolute minimum when they have so much capital invested in vehicles. Magirus produce a good truck that gets no more than its fair share of maintenance problems, but where it scores is in the availability of spares and fast fitting service."

Those are the two points which he had in mind when he put his mobile spares and workshops on the road, in a further effort to minimise customers' down time. In most cases they have equipment on board that will mean repairs can be effected immediately without the need for expensive tows to static workshops. The workshop is open seven days a week and likewise the spares department, both with a 24 hour call out system if required. They effectively cover the whole of East Anglia down towards the London docks and then up the coast as far as Lowestoft and Yarmouth. "We try to limit our sales to an area in which we are able to provide a full maintenance service. We have sold a lot of tippers in the Cambridgeshire area and a number

of the vehicles we have sold during the last three years have already clocked over .25 million miles, which proves they must be pretty reliable." John continued. All the mechanics working on the trucks have had specialist training with Marigus Deutz, so they can quickly get to the root of any problem in these air cooled engines, a full range of which are available from stock at Great Easton from a 50 tonne tractor unit to the light weight trucks under three tonnes gross weight.

As a further service to the haulage industry, John Parradine created Nett Hite Ltd., which stands for North Essex Truck and Trailer Hire. Currently Nett Hire has available 50 trailers, six Magirus tractor units, six light weights and twelve cars and estate cars. They are also in the process of opening a second base for the hire fleet at Rayne Road, Braintree, which has so far been running for just two years and is still expanding. There is a great demand for hire fleets on both long term contract hire and also short term daily or weekly self drive hire.

The expansion of the hire fleet is part of the planned expansion of the company in all three divisions. However, John Parradine is emphatic that he wants to see the company continue to be a "family business". "I regard all the people who work for me as part of the family. People must be really involved otherwise they will not have any regard or concern for the business," he went on. Although he intends to make the company stronger it will not be at the expense of his customers for his haulage, sales, maintenance or hire businesses. As far as John Parradine is concerned, one very old fashioned business maxim still holds true today: "the customer is always right and the most important factor in any business, without them we have no business, so it is our job to make them happy."

Magirus dealer John Parradine and Trans UK had a good working relationship, and they capitalized on this for advertising.

An annual growth rate of 50 per cent and a turnover of over two million pounds that is Trans U.K.

With a lifetime or experience in the haulage industry behind him, Bob Carter, in just seven years, has built an empire in freight handling which already has an annual turnover in excess of £2 million. As chairman and managing director of Trans U.K. Holdings and five operating companies, Bob is a very busy man. He is never too busy, however, to spend a night down at the docks checking the loading or un-loading of their customers' shipments. He is a firm believer in seeing a job through to its conclusion, which is one reason why he spends as much as four months out of every year overseas. Bob flies to foreign ports to continue his personal supervision of the work undertaken by his companies. This attention to detail by him and, indeed, his whole staff is one of the reasons for their continued success in all kinds of freight handling, particularly in the Middle East where they have been operating without incident for four years.

Bob first started earning his living in the haulage industry driving for his father's company, W. Carter Haulage at Melton. Then came a period in the R.A.S.C., where he studied engineering, followed by a return to the family business for another five years. By that time he had decided to branch out alone and began working for Sea Wheel Container Lines as a driver, working his way up eventually to take charge of the whole of their United Kingdom haulage operation. In 1970 Bob decided the time was ripe for him to begin in business on his own account. He set up Trans U.K. Containers toward the end of that year, operating strictly as a transport clearing house. Having no vehicles of his own he moved loads by using sub-contract hauliers, until he started his own company (Trans U.K. Haulage Ltd.) in 1973, with a small fleet of tractive units and trailers.

With the move into haulage Bob Carter was firmly established on the road to success, which has since led to his companies expanding at an annual rate of 50 per cent. Continuing his expansion programme he launched Trans U.K. Continental in 1974, to move cargo from the Continent to the Middle East. This was followed, in 1976, by Trans U.K.Forwarding.

"As a group we can offer clients a full service, moving anything from one kilo to 25,000 kilos world wide. We also offer repair, maintenance, forwarding, customs clearance, warehousing, in fact any facet of freight handling," Bob explained to *Intalink*. Since they began operations, Trans U.K. have handled all types of cargo, from the shipment of a complete antiques collection for the British Museum worth £2.5 million, to a cargo of cement to the Middle East, where the transport costs outweighed the real value of the goods. Although they have world wide insurance cover for all types of cargo, the only limitations being those imposed by ship-ping lines, they have never yet had to abandon a load, or indeed suffered a major breakdown, while operating in the Middle East.

This good record is, Bob believes, largely due to the reliability and experience of his 25 drivers. Unfortunately, to get drivers of the calibre required, Trans U.K. have found it necessary to institute their own training scheme, as those offered by Road Transport Training do not fit the bill. Another factor in their trouble free record is the company's fleet of modern long distance vehicles; unfortunately all foreign, being mainly Fiat with some Magirus Deutz, M.A.N. and Volvo, which are all fully equipped with extra fuel tanks, snow chains, extra lights, sun visors and cookers. Keeping the group's vehicles in top condition is the responsibility of Norman Harrison, who is the fleet engineer or Trans U.K., and his three trained fitters. Currently their work entails all maintenance and repairs on the group's vehicles and trailers.

Operating in the domestic transport field, handling about 500 cargo movements monthly throughout the U.K., is the container company with which Bob started. This side of the group operations is controlled by director John Joyce. John Scott is the director in charge of Trans U.K. Haulage, who from their Felixstowe depot operate 30 trucks and 50 trailers, providing a comprehensive system of UK and Continental and International haulage. Their field of operations extends throughout this country, Western Europe, Scandinavia, all the Middle East and the Balkan countries including Turkey and Greece. The remaining two companies within the group are Trans U.K. Continental and Trans U.K. Forwarding. The former, under the direction of Tony Waugh, operates a twice weekly, or as necessary, driver accompanied groupage service from the main towns in the U.K. to West Germany. Also this company deals with all the documentation and takes responsibility for sales and all other overseas operations of the group. To promote their own efficient customs clearance and forwarding services they use Trans U.K. Forwarding, which is controlled by Philip Greenfield. His service is also available for deep sea shipments to Australia and the United States.

Completing the total office workforce of seven are Graham Carter, director and company secretary, and Mary Giles. Together these two are able to handle the whole of the accounts, purchasing and sales operation, helped to some extent by hired computer time. The wide ranging interests of Trans U.K. are handled expertly and efficiently by this hard working team, who no doubt take their example from Bob Carter. He runs a tidy depot (a yard foreman, assistant and maintenance boy being employed to keep it that way) and a friendly office. Two qualities which have led to satisfied customers and staff; he loses very few of either!

63

across the yard. Learning from this, the next trailer that came back, he hatched a plan. Parking one side of the trailer on top of a railway sleeper to put it at an angle, and poised with any type of bottle or receptacle he could muster, he managed to drain what was left out of the trailer! Even Mary's typewriter case was pressed into action to collect the 'Gratis Vin'!

Tony Quinn, who traded as Quinn International, also gave Bob a lot of work from the Bacardi boats that arrived from Jamaica. All the Bacardi was destined for Three Mills Bond in east London. Being essentially a raw product, this Bacardi was about 150 per cent proof, not something you would want to have a big slug of! As with the wine trailers, there were often dregs left inside after the pumping out process. Once again, upon arriving back at the yard, the trailer would be jacked up by way of lifting the front end with the forklift and draining out what was left! After some time, however, the Bond began to refill the trailers with water (Trans UK was not the sole haulier of the Bacardi, it should be pointed out). Had it been tipped off about what people were up to? No one can know for sure, but this spelled the end of a free tipple of Bacardi.

WHAT THE DRIVERS HAVE TO SAY

PAUL ROWLANDS

There really is not much more that I can add about Paul Rowlands that is not already known. His autobiography, *Not All Sunshine and Sand*, documents his life as a driver and his voyages to the Middle East for Trans UK. However, his input and help with this book have been priceless, and not to acknowledge him so would be wrong, I feel. I owe him a debt of gratitude (and probably a bottle of whisky!) for all the help and time he has given me.

MICHAEL PRIGG

Michael Prigg was one of Trans UK's Afghanistan and Pakistan specialists. And, as were a lot of Bob's men, he was adept with the tools too, as Mick Coombes recalls.

"I can remember on one trip to Iran we had problems in eastern Turkey, a few miles outside of Erzurum. One of the wheel bearings on the trailer got very hot and seized on the stub axle. After waiting ages for it to cool down (which wasn't easy as the temperature was about 35 degrees), 'Priggy' came along and stopped as he normally would. I can remember his words now: 'Put the kettle on, and make some food, I am ruddy starving, and I will get the tools out and overalls on,' so that's what I did; he liked to be in control.

"After what seemed about six hours, lots of banging, shouting and swearing, plus lots of coffee laced with Slivovitz (plum brandy), the bearing was off, leaving a stub axle looking the worse for wear. Mick carried an air grinder in his truck, so we hooked that up to the air tank on his lorry, and after a long while it started to look like a stub axle again.

"After a few hours' sleep, we set off to Erzurum to find another bearing. Eventually we found two that he thought would do, but the company who had them did not want to sell them to us as they wanted to do the repair themselves.

They finally conceded, and sold them to us. Heading back to the truck, I said, 'Will it work?' He said. 'Have faith, of course it will.'

"After a long while of filing and grinding, he got the bearing to fit tight, greased it up, the wheel back on, one final cup of coffee and a meal, and we were on our way. We stopped every twenty minutes or so to see if it was running hot. We finally made the border at Bazagan, cleared customs, then on our way to Tehran. What a journey!"

Sadly Mick required a lung transplant in 2013, which was not successful, and he passed away on 22nd April that year.

KEITH WILLIAMS

Keith was another man with a sense of wanderlust.

"I moved to Felixstowe from Whitstable, Kent, in the summer of 1979 as I thought I would have a much better chance of achieving my life ambition of becoming an international truck driver. The only thing lacking was an HGV licence.

"Within a couple of weeks I'd secured a job in the workshops of United States Lines as a trailer fitter, but I realized within a week that this wasn't the career I was destined for and started visiting local hauliers to see if they'd be interested in taking on a trainee driver. Trans UK was one of the companies whose door I knocked at, and a couple of days later I received a call, asking me to come in for a chat.

"Bob Carter agreed to give me a start on a trial basis, to see if I was made of the right stuff.

"I started by shunting containers from Felixstowe dock in and out of Trans UK's yard. In those early days a HGV licence wasn't required to drive on the docks as it was private land.

"The truck I drove was an old ERF, but on occasions I would get to drive one of the road vehicles. The V10 left-hand drive Magirus Deutzs were my favourites and it hadn't really dawned on me at that time the historical significance of these trucks, the fact that they had covered thousands of miles travelling to and from the Middle East.

"I worked as a shunter for six months when I finally got the news that I had passed my probationary period, and I was to be sent to Road Transport Training at Mendlesham for a two-week course to gain my HGV1.

"On Friday, 2nd November 1979 I passed my test, and on the Monday I was given a truck of my own, a Fiat 130, and was sent up the road. I have never looked back and it was all down to Bob Carter having the confidence in me and seeing my potential. I can never thank him enough and to this day he is one of the best bosses I have ever worked for.

"Bob, along with the rest of the employees, from office staff to drivers, were a pleasure to work with. Bob would always make time to say hello and listen to you.

"I remember when we moved from Shaw Lovell's yard up to a piece of ground opposite the tobacco bond. It was a dust bowl in the summer and a huge muddy puddle in the winter. I was in the yard with John 'Sadie' Thompson, also known as Gypsy John. Another young driver called Kim Gladwell was told to pick up a Trans UK tilt trailer that had stood in the yard for several weeks and take it to the workshops at Capel St Mary. Kim came roaring down the yard towards John and I, kicking up clouds of dust, when John said to me, 'You watch this, I'll slow this lunatic down!' Well, he stepped in front of Kim's truck and yelled, 'Stop you idiot!' holding his hand up as he did so, and Kim came to an abrupt halt just in front of him.

"John turned to me, and started to say something, but before he could utter a word, the accumulation of several weeks' rain came gushing off the top of the trailer, straight over Kim's cab and soaked him from head to foot! He stood there speechless, and then shouted, 'I'll kill him!' With that, Kim hastily reversed back up the yard, swung round and made a sharp exit from the other gate. I was crying with laughter!"

JOHN 'TAFFY' DINWIDDY

John 'Taffy' Dinwiddy was the only driver to pass away while the company was running. Driving through the West Midlands, he suffered a heart attack at the wheel and crashed his truck. His body was thrown from the cab through the roof of a factory below the motorway.

John 'Taffy' Dinwiddy's tragic death made the local papers.

BRIAN WALES

Brian was born in 1938 and grew up in Bury St Edmunds, Suffolk. Brian's mum told his wife Maria that as a small boy, Brian would pinch his mum' s rolling pin to use as a gear stick, and a round breadboard for an impromptu steering wheel. He would sit outside on the doorstep making engine noises, steering, gear jamming and dreaming of the road!

Leaving school in 1955, it wasn't until 1961 that he started his first driving job. After a succession of various jobs, both local and long distance, in 1969 Brian went to work for Mitchell–Rowlands at nearby Buxhall. It was moving Claas combine harvesters from King's Lynn docks to the Claas UK HQ at Saxham. It was hard work, the combines had no power steering or batteries fitted, and the Ford D series truck he was driving was not really up to the job. When the Claas work slowed down, Brian had nothing to do so Mitchell–Rowlands sent him to subcontract for Trans UK doing container work, which took him as far as Ireland.

Brian enjoyed working for Bob, the work ethos suited him. He was then offered a long distance trip. He had to load up a consignment of pianos, which had all been collected in the east end of London. They were destined for a small village in the mountains near Turin in Italy. He jumped at the chance, taking his wife along too for the experience. They couldn't believe the hospitality of the Italians when they arrived. The man receiving the pianos got all his friends and family round to help unload, Brian and Maria weren't allowed to touch a thing! Then they were invited in for a huge meal and the alcohol flowed into the small hours.

> *Having a small cab did not bother me, I was quite happy bedding down on the shelf in the 86 cab.*

Brian decided to ask Bob for a job. He wanted to focus on going to the Middle East as he could earn more than just doing container work around England. His first steed was a hand-me-down Volvo F86. At the time it was the best vehicle Brian had ever driven. It was quiet and comfortable with such a smooth gear change. "I'm only a little fella," Brian laughs. "Having a small cab did not bother me, I was quite happy bedding down on the shelf in the 86 cab."

By comparison, he was not a fan of the F88. He did a trip to Germany in one when the regular driver was on holiday and didn't feel at home in it. He struggled to reach the foot pedals and to actually see out the windscreen. Brian soon found that being away from his wife and two sons for up to six weeks at a time was a challenge; it wasn't doing his marriage any good. His brother-in-law had a key cutting business and he suggested Brian should have a go at that and promptly sold him a key cutting machine. In 1978 he took a stall at Eye Sunday market and was amazed to take £76 on his first day – more than a week's wages he was earning as a driver! He had to keep driving trucks for regular income, but eventually thought that the key business could generate enough income to support him and his family and so he gave up driving. Although people said it would not last, Brian kept at it until he retired.

MICK COOMBES

Mick Coombes was born in Norwich, where he lived until the family moved south to Ipswich. Leaving school aged 15 in the summer of 1961, he started as a trainee butcher working in a shop for the Co-op on Chantry Estate. The first seeds were sown for a career as a driver as he moved roles within the Co-op, and became a driver's mate aged 17. He wasn't earning enough money at the Co-op and so he started job hunting. In 1966, Mick gained his first driver's job at an Ipswich bakery. Driving a Commer Karrier van around the town, he was delivering bread and cakes from the bakery to the shops. After four months, though, he decided it wasn't for him – eating too many doughnuts wasn't doing his figure any good. "I couldn't get out the bloody van door," Mick chuckles. After a brief spell as a taxi driver, Mick saw an advert from haulier H.C. Wilson of Elmswell and in August 1967, aged 21, he had his first lorry, a Bedford TK four-wheel rigid. The job entailed nationwide deliveries of Ipswich-built agricultural machinery. Mick enjoyed the variety of the work; he would usually unload himself at the dealerships. Mick had two years with H.C. Wilson and left in 1969.

I couldn't get out the bloody van door

After a string of various truck driving jobs, including some runs to the Middle East, as well as the odd flirt with taxi driving, Mick went to see Bob Carter for a job in the summer of 1974. His experience made him an obvious choice and Bob found a slot for him within a week. His first vehicle with Trans UK was a Volvo F86. Perhaps it is better Mick cannot recall for sure which one he had because the previous driver had particularly smelly feet! Even after Mick had cleaned it thoroughly, the aroma was left in the cab and it wasn't pleasant. Mick's first job was to go to Istanbul loaded with second-hand tractors. The job went like clockwork. He reloaded bicycles at Sarajevo, Yugoslavia, and came back to England.

From the Volvo, Mick moved into a brand new Fiat 619 named Cawsand Caliph. It was originally registered as REX 605R then re-registered as WVG 311S. For its first year it never displayed a British tax disc for the simple reason that it was never in the UK! Bob wanted him to have a Magirus Deutz when he acquired one as it had a bigger cab, and so Mick moved into PAL 525R, named Dartmoor's Redwing. For the mid-1970s they were huge in comparison to what other hauliers were operating.

Bob didn't actually know until we started writing this book that all the original four Fiat 619s he had bought had paid a visit to a mechanic in Turkey. For some cash the mechanic there, who was well versed with Fiats, took the baffles out of the exhausts and tweaked all the fuel pumps. Diesel at the time was between two and four pence a litre in places. It ruined the truck's economy but after being doctored they were different vehicles and literally would pull a house down. The Magirus did have a bigger cab to live in and the engine pulled like a train, although this one was factory fresh!

Mick had a rather unfortunate experience in Romania. He had successfully delivered to Istanbul, and was in Romania to load for the UK. It was winter. Snow, and the narrow cobbled streets in a town, made this a challenging drive. He heard two loud bangs as he went down a street, but he pressed on to the factory nearby and went to sleep parked outside the gates. In the morning, he dropped his tailgate and backed on a bay ready to load. Mick had gone to the office for a coffee, when a bemused loader came to find him and stated that they couldn't load the trailer as he already had cargo inside. Inspection showed the problem: Mick had hit a veranda on a house, which explained the loud bangs. It had knocked it clean off and it had gone through the roof of his trailer, complete with awning and washing hung on the concrete plinth with metal struts. It did work to Mick's advantage though; the manager at the factory bought it from Mick, and he fitted it on to his own house! His staff repaired the broken boards in the trailer and the sheet on the roof for free.

Mick then had a year working as the Felixstowe yard foreman under transport manager John Joyce. Mick's first marriage had failed and he had a new partner and so he wanted to be home more to spend some time with her. He didn't get on very well with John, and after six years at Trans UK he decided to leave in the summer of 1980.

Although it's nearly thirty-five years since he left Trans UK, he and a few others still meet Bob on a Wednesday to have a meal and a chat. After five decades of driving so many different sized vehicles and visiting so many places he still thinks the Maggie he used to drive was the best truck he has ever had.

MICHAEL LILLIE

Mick was born in 1941 in Bury St Edmunds, Suffolk and soon moved to Sudbury, just a few miles south. Aged 18, he went to Colchester on the train with a mate for a day out and they ended up getting drunk. Wandering back to the station to go home, they passed the Army recruitment centre and decided to go in to take the mickey out of the desk sergeant. However, the sergeant had the last laugh. Although not recalling it, three weeks later Mick received his call-up papers. In his drunken haze he had signed up to do a six-year stint in the Army, and had to report to Britannia Barracks in Norwich, where he joined the Norfolk Regiment.

Once he had served his time in the Army, his gained his first job as a lorry driver. A friend of his was driving for a haulier called Cousins, which was based at nearby Sible Hedingham, and he secured Mick a job there. After a string of driving jobs, as well as gaining his HGV1 licence, Mick joined Mitchell–Rowlands of Buxhall. Driving a Ford D800 tractor unit coupled to a low-loader with a four in line knock out axle, he was also engaged on the same combine harvester work as

Brian Wales. As with Brian, in 1974 Mitchell–Rowlands had no work for Mick. He rang Bob Carter to see if he needed anyone. Mick drove down in his car and was given one of the Volvo F86s for what should have been a few days just to earn some wages. Mick ended up leaving Mitchell–Rowlands and going to work for Bob full time, initially on UK work. After some time in Bob's employ, Mick booked a holiday, but, after a few days of the terrible British weather, he decided to go home early. When they got home, he rang Bob to see what he was doing on the following Monday. "You're going to Istanbul" was Bob's reply. Mick was taken aback, he'd never been abroad in a truck! Bob said he would be fine, Taffy was going as well and they could run together and he could show him the ropes.

Mick was taken aback, he'd never been abroad in a truck!

"Have you got a passport?" Bob asked. "No, I haven't," was the reply. "Well you'd better get one sorted."

And so on the Friday, Mick got some photographs taken and went up to Peterborough to the passport office and explained the situation. He had to wait four hours, but he came away with a temporary passport that lasted six months. The reason for only a temporary issue was he had not got his photographs signed as a true likeness. His first trip was indeed running with Taffy, which helped to dispel some of the nerves. They were both loaded with old Massey Ferguson tractors. In all, Mick only did four trips to Turkey. Nothing fazed him, and he would have happily gone further south if given the opportunity.

Mick was given a brand new Fiat 170 tractor unit named Cosden Tomboy. He settled into a regular job delivering and loading groupage at Gunter Bauman's in West Germany. Mick loved his Fiat, describing it as 'a great motor'. It had a lovely wide bed. He also earned the nickname 'Cowboy' while running abroad for Bob as he had a very expensive ornate pair of cowboy boots that were actually made in Dallas, Texas.

Trans UK had an annual Christmas party, which were the best of Mick's life. With a good boss and equipment, and a good crew of work colleagues, life was good. When the first rumours that the end of Trans UK was imminent, Mick unofficially got as many of the drivers as he could together for a meeting. He proposed to them that they would work for free for a month and be paid at a later date. After all, they had been earning good money, and they all loved their jobs. Only one driver said no, but he soon changed his mind. Mick took the idea to Bob, which he appreciated greatly, but sadly the problems had gone too far, and deferring wages for a month would not be enough to help the situation. Going on to pastures new was not a joyous thought.

Even now, after more than fifty years in employment, Mick views Bob Carter as the best boss he has worked for, and looks back at his days at Trans UK fondly.

TERENCE LUDAR 'SMUDGER' SMITH

"I didn't want to be a truck driver, I wanted to be a tower crane driver!" says Smudger chuckling. After getting out of the Army and becoming a truck driver, and after working for a few different companies, in 1974 Smudger was working for J.W.H. Spicer at Cambridge pulling trailers out of Felixstowe, and after a period of time it became a subcontractor for Trans UK, just doing its UK work.

One regular job it was doing for Bob was taking containers to Melton Mowbray, day and night. "We used to go to Pedigree Pet Foods at Melton Mowbray, weigh the box in at the factory, then drop the trailer and box in the BRS depot, collect an empty one, weigh it back out and back to Trans UK's yard, swap again and head back for the day man to do the same run.

> *I didn't want to be a truck driver, I wanted to be a tower crane driver!*

"At this time I was pestering Bob for a job, but he kept saying no as he didn't want to poach drivers. Anyway, I pestered and pestered away, and eventually Bob caved in, said to quit my job where I was and come and see him. I'll never forget it. I was starting on 1st December 1975 and Terry Blakesley would be going with me in another truck. I had just had a week at home, and my wife turned around the day I was setting off saying she wanted a divorce! I couldn't believe it, and said we will talk about it more when I get back, and off I went.

"My first trip was to Turkey in a Volvo F86 loaded with second-hand tractors. The trip went through to Koln, and on to the freight train. The train trip, which took you through West Germany due to permit restrictions, luckily passed uneventfully. We got through to Bulgaria, and that was where I had my first problem! The only way of locking a door on a Volvo F86 is to wind the window down, lock the door from the outside with the key and do the window back up. Well, in the middle of the night I got out the truck to answer a call of nature, and the door shut behind me, I was locked out!

"I sheepishly woke Terry up, who wasn't too impressed! There is a hole where the gear stick goes that you can get your arm through and get to the door handle, to unlock the door, but first we had to jack the cab up. 'Don't let it happen again,' warned Terry. 'I won't, don't worry,' was my reply. Well guess what happened the very next night? 'Terry, Terry . . .?' He wasn't amused, but helped me back in, but told me if it happened again he would leave me outside for the night!

"We went through the border at Kapicule, and into Turkey and we parted company after Istanbul. I set off across the Bolu Mountain, and worked my way down to the 'Telex Motel' at Ankara. The following morning, the motel spoke to the customer on my behalf, and they came and met me at the motel and took me to where I was unloading. At the time, we were collecting 10,000 deutschmarks for the haulage. Now when I got there, the people took all my paperwork, and went off without a word; this was all new to me, of course. I sat there all day wondering if they had just scarpered with my paperwork and maybe had me over! Anyway, eventually, at about 9pm, they returned. 'Where the hell have you been?' I shouted. Turns out they couldn't get hold of any deutschmarks in Ankara, so they had gone off to Istanbul to collect the money. 'You could have at least told me!' By this time I just wanted to get going and make up a bit of lost time, so I set off in the dark back over Bolu.

"I had a reload in Yugoslavia, 21 tonnes of aluminium blocks back to England. It was right up an extinct volcano where I had to go. It was beautiful, but not ideal in a truck. Once loaded I headed for home, and because of various hold-ups and having to do customs at every border, I managed to catch the last ferry home on Christmas Eve, which docked at midnight on Christmas morning. Well, I got off the ferry, did my customs checks, and Bob was waiting for me, along with his yard man and my wife. Well, as soon as my wheels started turning she came haring through like a battleship in full sail, crying, 'Don't leave me Smudge, don't leave me!'

"I said, 'What are you on about; it was you wanting to leave me!' So all was well that ended well.

"I spent about nine months doing just Greece and Turkey. I met some fantastic people while doing it. I wanted to go further, but Bob wouldn't send the old F86s any further than that. Well, eventually one day I got back after a trip, and Bob asked me if I would mind having a short break, as he had a new truck for me. I got a lift from Paul Rowlands to Stowmarket, and I picked up my new truck, a MAN 232 column change. I'll never forget the registration number: SUV 719N! I was king of the road now! So I drove down to Felixstowe, back to the yard and saw Bob.

I spent about nine months doing just Greece and Turkey. I met some fantastic people while doing it.

"'Where am I off to now with this then Bob?'

"'Kuwait,' was his answer.

"Well my jaw almost hit the floor! Once again I shipped out, and aside from the usual delays it was pretty uneventful down into Turkey. There was a saying on the old Middle East route: at Ankara, turn right for the Arab states and turn left for Iran, Afghanistan and Pakistan. Bob's usual policy was that for the first couple of trips you would run with at least one other truck, but I was on my own for this one. Luckily for me, I met up with a man called John who was working for Astrans at the time. He was going the same way as me, and so he was showing me what he could to help me along the way. We got through Syria and down into Jordan, and that's where you then go across what's known as H4, which is literally across the desert and through to Saudi Arabia, following oil drums filled with sand. It was about 150km into the desert where you would find the police station and the first part of customs. Once through there you drive through some of no man's land and on to the next part of customs, which was another 150-odd kilometres. At that point you then turn on to tarmac road, and follow the famous TAP line (Trans Arabian Pipeline), which goes across Saudi Arabia. At the end was a truckstop and services, which had been nicknamed 'Watford gap', where everyone would stop for a coffee and a chat, and a bit further along was the Kuwait border and the convoys of trucks that they put you in for some reason.

"Talk about coals to Newcastle, I was loaded with carpets for Kuwait city! We cleared customs quite quickly, and we had to stay in a hotel at the border as you were not allowed to stay in your truck in the compound overnight. It took all day to unload the truck, but once I was empty I was straight back to the border, because if you're empty you don't have to travel in one of the convoys. I ran back empty all the way to Yugoslavia, reloaded and headed home. I did the whole trip in seventeen days! Sadly, I was the only person to do Kuwait as the customer never paid Bob for the job."

> *Talk about coals to Newcastle, I was loaded with carpets for Kuwait city!*

GERRY KEATING

Gerry Keating was quite a latecomer to the haulage industry. "I wanted a change of direction when I was 45. I had a love of sailing and travel, and transport seemed to be the right choice as I could get paid to travel. I put myself through my class one test (Gerry was already a qualified PSV driver), but I was then up against the age old problem of 'no experience, no job' so I ended up signing up with an agency to get some experience, and managed to get some work doing sugar beet to the Ipswich factory. I had been to see Bob about a job, and got on well with his secretary, as she was also keen on boats. He didn't have a job at the time, but we seemed to have built up a good rapport, and he was pleased to hear that I had European experience from the coaches, and that I also had language skills, which I have always had an interest in.

"Soon after our meeting, I got a call from Bob because a job vacancy had come along, which he offered to me, and so I began at Trans UK. To start with I was on container work around the UK, building up my experience, and learning from my mistakes. After about two months, Bob said to me that he had a truck that was stuck in Belgrade and would I go out and rescue it? I was to go in a truck with another driver, collect the stricken vehicle and carry on with it down to Turkey.

"We got to the National Hotel in Belgrade, which was a regular stop for western trucks on the route at the time. The truck's mirrors had been stolen along with a few other items, but we managed to get the truck started and safe to go and we set off. The truck was loaded with tractors, which I got delivered, reloaded the truck and got it back without incident to Felixstowe. When I got back, Bob asked me what I thought of it, and I told him it was almost as good as sailing! That was me then as his newest international driver.

"After some time I got offered a run to Pakistan. I was then in my element. I was on my own, making my own decisions and travelling. Speaking nine different languages was a distinct advantage.

"One trip I was with another driver called Malcolm Howe (nicknamed Shit up a Tree!), we were heading back empty, and we were around Lahore. The road was very busy with people, animals and cars, and there were also lots of trees that were overhanging. Now I had been keeping a close eye on them, but Malcolm must have missed one as I heard an almighty BANG! I looked in my mirror, and it looked like I had a barrage balloon following me! Well we stopped to take stock of what had happened, and unfortunately, the scene started to turn a bit ugly. Fortunately the local police arrived on the scene. One man alleged that Malcolm had run him over and broken his leg. The policeman asked him which leg was broken but he couldn't decide! Well, we were soon on our way, and we got the trucks to Kabul, and there we stripped the trailer down to repair it so we could carry on and reload the trucks."

LENNY BALAAM

It is fair to say that Lenny has had a deep interest in all things mechanical since he was a young boy. Born in Rattlesden in 1941, he purchased his first vehicle when he was 12 years old. He bought a BSA 600 side valve motorcycle, which had a side-car attached. Len didn't want the sidecar, and told the seller to either take it off, or he wouldn't have it. It cost him just £6. It was a large machine for a 12-year-old! This was to have a great influence on the rest of his life. He was fascinated how it worked and loved to take it apart and reassemble it. He learnt he had an aptitude for all things mechanical and eventually sold it on at a profit. Len left school aged 15 and decided to try a military lifestyle, so he joined the Grenadier Guards. He completed all the hard work of training at Pirbright, near Guildford in Surrey. He wanted to be a dispatch rider on a motorcycle but he never became one. He soon had enough of the discipline and bought himself out to return to civvy street. Although Lenny never took an HGV test in his life, driving trucks or repairing them was to become the main thread throughout his working life. His first driving job was with W. G. Harvey at Rickinghall. It had cattle floats and rigids for carting fresh peas off the fields, which were hauled to Lowestoft for podding at the Birds Eye factory.

Lenny then went to drive for Jacobs Transport from Hunston, Suffolk. Here Lenny drove a green ERF LV articulated unit. He wasn't supposed to, but he used to often sleep in it although it had no curtains and was only a day cab. Lenny liked the vehicle. It would pull well having a 180hp Cummins engine. It was in this truck Lenny had a horrendous crash, the only one of his entire career, and it nearly cost him his life. At the time Pilkington's Glass Factory at St Helens was on strike and a lot of glass was being imported from Belgium to cope with demand. He picked up a tilt trailer from Felixstowe quay destined for Liverpool, where customs clearance would be obtained. Then he would run it to Rochdale for delivery. The trailer was customs sealed, which meant he couldn't look inside when he picked it up. Once he had set off, he thought it handled rather badly. It transpired that 19 tons of glass had been loaded on the back of the trailer, and the front part was empty. The accident happened on the A428 between St Neots and Bedford. While negotiating a bend the load shifted and tipped the whole unit and trailer over. It transpired that the load had not been secured, but with a customs seal on, he was not able to check this before leaving. The cab completely disintegrated and it ended up on its side lying in some trees. He was very lucky to get out, although his right arm still shows the scars.

Lenny had since changed jobs yet again, to a company called Burroughes and Dunn, when he had an inkling things were going wrong with it. Based at Orsett, he worked out of Felixstowe port pulling containers. He knew of Bob Carter from when he had subcontracted work to his first employer, W. G. Harvey, when Bob was at Seawheel. Although Len never worked for Bob directly then, as he was kept busy on the meat side, he knew who he was and how he operated. At that time Bob had a small office in the Crane Fruehauf building in Walton Avenue, just outside the docks. Lenny heard on the grapevine that Bob was getting some trucks, and called in to see him to ask if he would need any drivers. The outcome of the conversation was positive. When the first new Volvo F86 finally turned up, Bob said he could give him a start. True to his word, when Duffields eventually delivered the first Volvo F86, Bob named it Cosden Major, put Len behind the wheel, and he was Trans UK's first employed driver. Lenny's first work for Bob was hauling Sea Land containers through C. Shaw Lovell. He once loaded a Sea Land container with whisky for export in Liverpool. He noticed a Leyland Sherpa van that kept driving around as he was loading. Feeling uncomfortable about it, Bob organized a police escort all the way to Felixstowe. A motorbike started the journey and different forces kept coming in and dropping out as he made his way south, all following at a distance just to check Lenny made Felixstowe safely.

> *It was really good fun, even if it was hard work most of the time*

Lenny also found Bob his second driver when the second new Volvo appeared, which was registered as SBJ 152M and named Cawsand Cavalier. Gwynne 'Ray' Rainham was Lenny's brother- in-law at the time, and Bob took him on to drive it. When Bob found his first Volvo F88, he offered it to Lenny as he was the longest serving driver. It was Lenny's idea to suggest that Charlie Frost at Needham Market could do all the warranty work on the new Volvos.

"It was because I had the F88 that I ended up on the first Middle East trip," recalls Len with a smile. "It was really good fun, even if it was hard work most of the time, and having Bob in the car made things that little bit smoother."

Back in England afterwards, Lenny was proud of the success of the first trip. When Bob discussed with him how it would work, they agreed that they would have at least a week at home before setting off again on another trip to Iran. Lenny's passport was stamped at Kapicule in ELU 922J on 6th June 1975 and again, in GPW 355N on 17th August 1975. Lenny was the only Trans UK driver who had done the trip already. He agreed to lead the other two novices when they left on the second convoy to Abadan in August 1975. There were times though when he wondered what had he done.

When they got home after the second trip Bob explained after a couple of days he wanted the three trucks to go back out again. Lenny did not want to go back so soon as he had a wife and two young sons he wanted to spend some time with. Len had a long think about what he wanted to do and decided to leave Trans UK. He joined Taylor Barnard based at Felixstowe on general haulage. This was not to last for too long, however, and Lenny came back to work for Bob as a mechanic based at the workshop in the Capel St Mary depot. He worked beside Peter Ainger for two years. Although Bob loved his Magirus Deutz trucks, Lenny thought they were no good. They were regularly blowing oil seals in the engine. Lenny thinks being air cooled caused the problem, as he was always replacing them.

At the time of writing in 2017, Lenny is now 75 and enjoying retirement, although he clearly misses the satisfaction of fixing something that is broken. He still had his small briefcase as a reminder of his two trips to Iran containing maps, paperwork and his passport. A special memory of an adventurous time.

PAUL DOODSON

"I first met Bob Carter after Terry 'Smudger' Smith took me down to Felixstowe one Saturday to meet him as I was looking for a job. Bob and I had a brief chat, and having told him about my work history, which was non-existent due to serving in the armed forces, much to my surprise I was told to come back the following Saturday, where I was given the keys to my first truck; as I recall it was a Fiat.

"After some months on containers, it seems I must have being doing something right as he sent me into Europe to do a delivery, and so it went from there.

"Bob gave me a chance in life and those steep learning curves and experiences taught me how to get myself out of trouble, both in the UK as well as working for companies in France after my time at Trans UK. I will be ever grateful to him for his faith in me and giving me a start, for I was a complete stranger with very little experience."

EDDY ENGLISH

Eddy first met Bob while he was working for Green and Skinner of Ipswich.

He was loading groupage from Bob's yard, and after two years of regularly going into the yard Eddy asked Bob for a job. Bob pointed to a Magirus Deutz parked in the yard and said, "You can drive that if you like." On arrival back at Green and Skinner's yard, a week's notice was duly given. There was holiday owing and Eddy was told to take his holiday as notice and thus could leave immediately. His Trans UK career started the following Monday with a multi-drop load of wine.

Eddy did a couple of continental trips for Bob but most of his career was UK-based. Bob asked Eddy to consider becoming Trans UK shop steward, a job that was taken on. They both had a mutual respect for each and never had a cross word. Any issues were discussed over a cup of coffee, and driver/employer relations were always good. Eddy describes Bob as a very good employer and a very good friend.

BERNIE MARTIN

Bernie worked for Bob as sub-contractor driver for Clover Transport. He first met Bob when he was driving for Page Brothers Transport of Capel, who were eventually bought out by Bob. The Page Brothers' yard became the Trans UK yard at Capel, which is just up the road from where the drivers and Bob met regularly for lunch.

They knew each other for forty-eight years, which is a long friendship by any standards. Bernie's first trip for Bob was to Iran with a back load of bicycles from Sarajevo when it was part of Yugoslavia. This first load was followed up by numerous others to Middle Eastern destinations such as Syria, Iran and Turkey.

During their long friendship they went through thick and thin together. At one time, Bob, Bernie and Chris Craven all lived in the yard at BSP Claydon – Bernie in his lorry, Bob in a caravan and Chris in an old Tesco trailer; the highs and lows of life in the transport industry!

JOHN OVERTON

John also worked for Clover Transport and drove a day-cabbed Scammell Crusader to the Middle East, no mean feat! They became firm friends, even taking holidays together, one of which was to America.

One of John's first jobs for Bob was to transport an over-length load of pipes from Felixstowe to Derby. Because of the way the pipes were loaded, it was not possible to put the twist locks in place. The decision was made to chain the load on, and off set John. He got as far as the Water Tower Roundabout on the edge of Felixstowe and the load came off. Bob to the rescue: the load was reloaded on to another trailer and John got to the delivery safely.

John's first trip abroad was to Istanbul, most of the loads that John did were to Turkey and the rest of the Middle East. Whilst a lot of the work was to the Middle East, John also undertook some UK only trips.

Following the demise of Trans UK, John operated some trucks of his own. These he had serviced and maintained by Bob, who was at this time running his garage business from Debach Transport premises.

MAURICE HORREX

Maurice and Bob both served in the army. Bob as a volunteer in the Royal Electrical and Mechanical Engineers (REME). Maurice served as a Grenadier Guard and this is his tribute to his friend and employer:

At ease soldier, your service is done
Farewell Soldier and Friend
Rest in Peace.

THE
AFTERMATH

IN 1979, TRANS UK HAD BEEN WORKING FOR A COMPANY called Meredith and Boreham Shipping, sending a lot of trailers unaccompanied to the Middle East from Felixstowe Docks. Unfortunately, it got into trouble when one of its boats docked in Sharjah docks. Bob had a feeling the company may have been getting into financial difficulty as it had been getting later with its payments to him for the work, but this had caught him by surprise. The ferry contained about a dozen Trans UK trailers along with some rental trailers that had been hired in.

"I spoke to our agent at the docks, and asked him to ensure that Abdulla Sari, the local haulier that we used in Dubai, got hold of all of our trailers including the rentals in lieu of payment for the haulage, so I could get this all sorted out. Our insurance policy had an 'abandonment clause' in it, for instances when the whole truck, trailer and load got abandoned en route. Fortunately this had never happened to us until this point. So I claimed on my insurance for the abandonment of my trailers in Dubai. The problem was, the insurance company wouldn't pay up on my claim for abandonment, so I wouldn't pay my premium when it came for renewal," recalls Bob.

This dragged on for some time, in fact for more than one year.

Then Bob got a letter through the post saying the insurance company was going to cancel the insurance policy, despite the fact it owed Trans UK the best part of £40,000.

"I was in trouble," says Bob.

"I spoke to a barrister, who looked through all the paperwork, and confirmed I was in the right. So I went to see the insurers in person at their offices, and explained what was what, and what had happened, but it all fell on deaf ears. Unknown to me, they had got me blacklisted by Lloyd's of London. So I decided to have a look around, and get insurance elsewhere to continue trading.

"I managed to get insured by a company called Deben Insurance, they were something to do with my families company, (W. Carter haulage), and so we were able to carry on as before. Then Deben Insurance told us that we had to pay our premium as a lump sum instead of instalments as Lloyd's of London had been on to them. Now I didn't think this would be a problem, so I went and saw the bank manager to arrange this so we could keep trading. Almost overnight the receivers were in the yard at Capel! To make matters worse, this all happened on my birthday, what a present! I looked into whether I could take this to the courts, but as it had dragged on and on I didn't have the funds to take them to court to contest it."

"The receivers had a good look around. It didn't take them long to realize that if they closed the doors, themselves and the bank could get their money and fees, and so that is what they did. In that last month that it was trading, Trans UK had made £29,000 profit on paper, and the overdraft in the bank was under £100,000, yet this did not seem to make any difference to the receivers, and the company ceased to exist.

"Once the dust had settled after Trans UK had ended, I managed to get myself an interim operator's licence so I could carry on with some work. I previously had made an agreement with my fuel supplier in Essex to take four of my Trans UK trucks as a payment for the fuel I had bought from them before the bank had closed us down. I arranged with them that when I bought fuel from them, I would pay a ha'penny more per gallon, to also cover anything else that was still owing from when Trans UK had been shut down."

Johnson Stevens Agencies was pleased to give Bob some work for his trucks. This was working out well, but unfortunately the other hauliers who were also working for it at the time did not like the fact that Bob was back working and just on a temporary licence. The other hauliers all got together and gave Johnson Stevens the ultimatum; either Bob goes, or the rest of the contractors will go elsewhere to work. As Bob recollects: "I had a call from Derek Johnson at home one night. He told me what was happening. I was offered to be the sole haulier for Johnson Stevens, Derek really appreciated our service and loyalty. But if I could not be the sole haulier, I would have to take my trucks off his work. His hands were tied in this situation. He couldn't take the risk of carrying on and face losing all his other subcontractors. Sadly, I didn't have anywhere near enough trucks for this to be possible and so, very reluctantly, I had to turn his offer down, and take my trucks off of their work."

It wasn't much after that when Bob received a letter from the licensing authorities saying they were not going to renew his licence.

Bob was at a bit of a loose end, and so he decided to go freelance. "I still had the workshop at the Capel yard due to it being owned by my father, and so I started to do some mechanical work from there for a few people I know. I couldn't run trucks as they had revoked my O licence. It kept me fairly busy, and my customer base expanded. I then took over some trucks from a man who owed me money and had just gone bankrupt. I spoke to the drivers of the trucks and told them that if they filled the trucks with diesel and brought them to me I would pay their wages. I even told the transport manager if he told me which finance companies owned which trucks I would also pay him his wages. So I had the trucks in my yard, and I spoke to the finance houses about getting the money owed to myself for maintenance, or as an alternative, to give me the truck as payment. This was the easiest option for them and so I ended up with six tractor units. As I had no operator's licence, I couldn't run them myself, and so I decided to just hire them out instead as I had a few customers who had the work but not the capital to purchase another truck."

After taking payment on a debt, Bob rented this V10-powered Maguris Deutz out to customer Orwell Transport.

W&D Maintenance's Scania 111 recovery truck. Converted from a tractor unit, it was this vehicle that was towing Bob dressed in his best wet weather gear to recover the stricken German Mercedes.

After an unusual request, Bob and the team at W&D rebuilt this MAN for use on overland travel to Africa.

Trying to warm up! The recovery of this accident-damaged, German-registered Mercedes required Bob to be dressed like a paint sprayer to try and keep himself dry and warm.

Cheer up Bob! Having a well-deserved beer while servicing Chris Craven's Volvo. More often than not, alcohol was generally used between the two of them to pay the bills. In fact Bob, cannot remember actually handing Chris an invoice for any work that he did!

Chris Craven's Volvo finally ready to hit the road after a year being built in the workshops at Debach.

In 1984, a man called Charlie Read was a good customer of Bob's. He was a second-hand truck dealer from Ardleigh in Essex. He came to visit one day as he had been offered the yard for sale. Well this was news to Bob! It seemed that his brothers had looked into selling the yard on behalf of their father, as he was the man who had put the money up when Bob originally bought out Page Brothers when Trans UK was going. Charlie had a look around, they had a chat and decided on a price, and the yard was sold on to him.

After cashing in a couple of life insurance policies to give him a little bit of capital, Bob decided to try starting a small import export line with Cyprus. "I knew that if I could fill containers with spare parts for cars and trucks, I could sell them on in Cyprus, and reload the boxes with either local produce or local crafts. I had a good friend called George Kolomydene from a company called IMM. He had also been the agent for Meredith and Boreham Shipping (who were the undoing of Trans UK), so I went and spoke to him about my idea. He thought it would be worth a go, so I decided to do a small shipment first as a trial run. I spoke to a haulier out in Cyprus who I had previously dealt with when dabbling with other work at Trans UK, and found out what spare parts for their fleet they were finding hard to buy. A lot of the parts were small ancillary things rather than actual panels or engines. So I bought a wooden box, perhaps 3ft square, and filled it with things like door handles, light lenses and the like, all smaller bits and pieces. I could just about lift the box by myself, so I took it to Heathrow airport, and flew with it myself out to Cyprus. I spoke to customs, went back and paid the import duty a few days later, and sold all the spares to the haulier when I arrived, and they were delighted! From this trial run I could see that there was potential in it."

When he got home, Bob went and saw a haulier called George Thorpe who was selling off some of his fleet. He purchased four complete AEC Mandator trucks, and a job lot of vehicle spares such as engines and tyres.

He thought it would be worth a go, so I decided to do a small shipment first as a trial run.

"I knew that they couldn't be exported complete, as there would be a lot of import duty on a complete working truck, and so the chassis was cut in half on each truck, and they were packed into two containers I had also purchased for this shipment. The idea was to start using the containers over and over on the same run. I filled all the paperwork out myself, and consigned it to myself at the hotel I was going to be staying at while I was in Cyprus. I would be using this hotel as an office while I set about selling off all the spares."

Then, once again, Bob had some bad luck.

"Once I got to Cyprus, George the agent had a big heart attack, and was placed into intensive care. I was sat there for several days, and the chances of him making a recovery were looking slim. Somehow, word got out that I had two containers of spares sat on the docks waiting, and it wasn't long before I had a phone call asking me if they were for sale. So I arranged to meet the caller at my hotel. As soon as I saw the man, my gut feeling was not to trade with him, I don't know why but I just had that instinct. So we had a chat about what I had, and I showed him the manifest of what spares I had, and he made me an offer that was far too low. I rejected his offer, and he told me that by law in Cyprus if the duty isn't paid for within a certain amount of time then the items would go to auction and that he would simply buy them there. I wasn't too fazed, as I already knew this was the case, but luckily for me, I knew a customs agent in Cyprus through some of George's family connections. I went and spoke to him about my predicament, and when I explained that all the paperwork was made out to myself at the hotel, he was very surprised! But, because I had done this, there wasn't anything that anyone could do about my containers as long as I was paying the dock fees. Eventually I waited in Cyprus for a month, sadly George wasn't getting any better and my money was starting to run low, so I decided to return my containers to the UK out of principle rather than sell all the spares for nothing. I obtained an export licence to return my containers.

> *I also decided while I was there that I may as well try and import something back to the UK.*

"I also decided while I was there that I may as well try and import something back to the UK. So I spoke to the shipping line about how much a 20ft container was to the UK and promptly ordered two of them, which I filled with pottery and other local crafts, and they went on the same ship as my returning spares. Once I got back to the UK, I easily sold the AEC spares, but the pottery and crafts took a bit longer to move on to garden centres and the like. All in all the potential was there but without my agent I was a bit stuck, so I decided to give up on the idea."

Upon his return, Bob relocated himself to nearby Claydon into a static caravan in W&D Maintenance's yard, another company with which he was friendly.

Two men ran W&D Maintenance, Graham 'Chalky' White and Ivan Davis. Bob started doing some work for them as a self-employed fitter from their yard. He

Working as a 'second man' required some out of gauge loads. The truck loaded from Sheffield Forgemasters these ships anchors for export from Felixstowe.

Bob on the right with his long-term friend, Jimmy Parker, sat behind the wheel of the forklift.

bought a Fiat van, which was equipped as a mobile repair van, and brought some of his customers from his days at Trans UK. General maintenance, servicing and also some recovery work were the normal jobs, although sometimes something a little different was offered to the team. They were approached one day by an American and a South African man to build them a truck with a difference. They wanted a truck built that could take passengers overland down to South Africa and back. They already had the basis for the truck, an old ex German army MAN. So the local scrapyards were raided for things such as fuel tanks, seats, etc, and the truck was converted. As far as Bob knows, it made it all the way to South Africa, as he never heard back from the pair.

Recovery jobs were also quite commonplace. W&D owned a Scania 111, which had been converted to a recovery truck. One particular job proved to be a chilling experience for Bob. There was a stricken German Mercedes–Benz that had to be towed back from Birmingham. The truck had been involved in an accident and was also a non-runner. Bob lost the toss of a coin and had to steer the Mercedes while Chalky drove the Scania. He had no lights, no power steering and no wind-screen! Dressed in full waterproof overalls and a mask, Bob had to endure rain all the way back home. To make matters worse, when they were within a few miles of their Claydon yard, Chalky started to fall asleep at the wheel. Bob couldn't do anything but hold on for dear life and hope that Chalky could make it back the last few miles. Thankfully he managed to stay awake for long enough to get them all safely home.

It was during this time that Bob met his good friend, Jimmy Parker.

The pair of them were approached by another friend of Bob's called Chris Craven. Chris was running a Volvo F12 truck to and from Germany and had just purchased a second one to put on the road. He asked Bob if he could do some conversion work and generally 'do it up' for him. There was no rush at all, he told them, and no spec to follow, just to surprise him.

Bob knew that Chris was a big fan of American trucks, and so he decided to try to use some of their influence on his truck.

Bob knew that Chris was a big fan of American trucks, and so he decided to try to use some of their influence on his truck. During a visit to his friend Derek at D.J. Spall's scrapyard Bob found a Granning lift axle from an unknown truck, and also a very large Volvo fuel tank. These were duly purchased for the new project. The axle itself needed very little altering to get it to fit. The fuel tank had to be mounted across the chassis to fit due to its size. Another purchase was an old fibreglass Ford transit van body that another friend had at his scrapyard. This was duly modified, and mounted on to the chassis to conceal the fuel tank and also provide storage for tool and spares, or even be used as somewhere to sleep if need be. An Iveco air kit was added to the roof for fuel efficiency, half of the grille was blanked off as it didn't actually provide the radiator with any cooling, and the truck was painted the same as Bob's work van, in black and grey with maroon stripes. The final touch was adding a strip of black masking tape down the window to make it look like it had a split windscreen! All in all the whole venture took just under a year to complete, and when Chris saw it he was over the moon with what Bob and Jimmy had created.

The final touch was adding a strip of black masking tape down the window to make it look like it had a split windscreen!

'ONE OF THOSE TRIPS!'

Bob also did quite a bit of work for a friend of his called John 'Hoppy' Green. Called Hoppy due to having one false leg, he did a lot of subcontract work for a company called MCL (Michael Cave Ltd). This work was mostly all 'out of gauge' or abnormal loads. If these needed a 'second man' (as required by law), Bob would accompany Hoppy. It was the Easter of 1987 and Hoppy had a delivery to Turkey, but Bob was required more for the speed of delivery as the load was not out of gauge, but was red hot urgent and needed desperately at the oilfield in Eastern Turkey.

The trailer was preloaded when they collected it from MCL's yard near Bedford. Being a stickler for paperwork, Bob soon noticed before they left that there was no permit for driving through Greece. Hoppy told him that it was to be collected at the Greek border when they arrived there.

The run went relatively smoothly down through Europe and through Yugoslavia until they got to the Greek border. The lack of a permit created a problem, and they were not allowed to carry on. They managed to get themselves to Thessaloniki airport to meet someone from DHL who had to fly out with a permit for them to carry on. This fiasco cost them two days. Due to this delay, when they arrived at the Greek–Turkish border, the border was swarming with both side's armies, and was as good as closed. The two countries were arguing over who owned the Greek-controlled islands off the Turkish coast again. This cost the pair another day in waiting while the countries settled their differences.

Once through the border and inside Turkey, they made their way to the famous Mocamp at Istanbul. The trailer had been suffering with overheating brakes, so they decided to call it a night at the Mocamp and have a quick check in the morning to see if there was anything causing the problem.

The following day, once satisfied that all was well, it was off towards Ankara, and then turn right towards the south of the country and over the Bolu mountain. The route Bob had suggested was Diyarbakir, Sukulu and on to the town called Batman. However, Hoppy overruled him and decided to take the most direct route according to the map. Bob tried in vain to convince Hoppy otherwise, but he wanted to try and make up some of the time that they had lost so far. After a

John 'Hoppy' Green loaded with a trailer for Belgium. The load is a machine that processes potatoes and fries them.

John 'Hoppy' Green strikes a pose with his Volvo F89.

Reversing on to the ferry from Hull for the night crossing to Zeebrugge.

Trying to squeeze into the factory in Belgium. The customer had specified a steering trailer due to the access available, but this request got lost along the way. Hoppy's driving skill managed to defuse the situation when he inched the trailer in without the need of a steering trailer.

In position to unload the machinery. Note the small locker on the chassis behind the cab, an addition that Bob had added on to the Volvo after finding it in a scrapyard. Normally used by Hoppy as a tool box, when Bob went with him he cleared it out and used it as his sleeping quarters!

Running repairs. Bob is seen here fixing a tyre on Hoppy's Ford Transcontinental in France en route to Milan. (Note the use of an old Trans UK tilt as a sheet for the load on the second picture).

Hoppy's Ford parked in Milan after delivering to an exhibition.

Loaded for the oilfields of Turkey.

Queueing at Ipsla; the Greek/Turkish border.

Time for a swap of drivers in Turkey.

Kicking up the dust in Turkey.

couple of hours' driving, the road condition had deteriorated enough so that they wanted to turn around and go back, but there simply wasn't anywhere suitable to turn themselves around. Onwards they pressed, and then they gained a passenger.

It was like John Travolta stood there hitching a lift, leather jacket, big quiff the lot!

"It was like John Travolta stood there hitching a lift, leather jacket, big quiff the lot! He got in and sat in the middle of the truck and we cracked on. We crested a hill further down the road, and there, right in front of us, is a magnificent white bridge that crossed the river that was also now in front of us! Oddly, the map didn't show any river at all. We decided to get on the bridge and cross this river, and hope for the best. Not too much longer after crossing the river, the truck gained a water leak, which we traced to a hose that had split. When we stopped to repair the truck, the locals didn't appear too friendly. I had previously been to Turkey dozens of times, but this was the only time I ever felt threatened as such. Thankfully, our passenger jumped out and spoke to the locals, who then left us alone. A local shop-keeper gave us some water for the truck, and all three of us were on our way again.

"When we finally got back on to a main road, it turned out to be the one I had suggested taking in the first place from Ankara!

"As we got close to where our delivery was destined for, we were trying to locate exactly where we had to go when a car went past the other way, which immediately stopped, turned around and flagged us down. There were two Americans from the oilfield in the car, and they had been out looking for us all day! They lead us to the oilfield site, which only had one access road in. We took a look at it, and we were frankly unsure if we could even get into the road, but it did, just!"

The following morning, the load was winched from the truck across on to one of their own trucks, and the duo were then off empty back towards Europe. The reload, which had been arranged, was from Bergamo in northern Italy, with another British owner–operator in a Volvo F10.

The load, destined for Kodak in Whitehaven, was not actually ready so they had to wait three days for the loads to be completed so they could get going. Once they were loaded and rolling, they then got stopped at the Mont Blanc tunnel to await an escort through due to being over length. As soon as they got out on the French side the French police would not allow them to continue, as it was a bank holiday weekend! They spent the night in the parking area at the top of the mountain, but Hoppy soon got fed up with that, and they sneaked down to the Centre Routier restaurant in Cluses at the bottom of the mountain and spent the weekend in there instead.

The rest of the run back up through Europe was uneventful, until they arrived at Dieppe docks. The problem there was that they couldn't actually load the trailer on to the ship with their truck; the load was too long and they didn't have enough ground clearance. They had to get a French dockworker with one of their Tugmasters to load the trailer on to the ship; it had better ground clearance and a raising 'fifth wheel', so could avoid the kerbs much more easily.

Once they finally got back into the UK, English customs happened to be on strike, and this final episode was enough to end the trip for the pair as Hoppy's truck was needed back for an MOT, so they dropped the trailer at Newhaven and went home.

Finding it difficult to stay out of transport, Bob decided to try once again in haulage when an opportunity came along. He was offered some local work for a truck through a local company called Debach Enterprises. Purchasing an Iveco cheaply, getting an O licence again, and also finding a driver, he was back in business of sorts. He called his new company Trans UK Roadhaul. The work was all out of Felixstowe, and only to one of three places; Ipswich, Bentwaters or Debach itself. Bob had been asked to help the family company out of a muddle at the time, and had gone back to the workshops after an absence of almost thirty years, although still on a self-employed basis.

They too also offered him some subcontracting haulage for themselves if he got another truck. So a second truck was sourced from a local pig farmer in Needham Market and put to work.

The trailers he used were both old tilt trailers from his friend Chris Craven, who had packed up in haulage at this point, stripped down to make flatbeds. The work started off well for the first few months, but the traffic planner at Debach did not like Bob from the start and made it difficult for him to make any money from the truck. "The Carter's work wasn't reliable enough either as I was the newest subcontractor there, so to speak, and so once again I had to get rid of the trucks."

The Carter's work wasn't reliable enough either as I was the newest subcontractor there, so to speak

In December 2001, Bob went into Papworth Hospital for a quadruple heart bypass. When he was sat with the consultant, the procedure was being explained

The famous Londra camp at Istanbul. Despite the decline of the amount of overland traffic to and from Arabia, it was still a well-known stopping point and a melting pot of trucks and drivers from far and wide.

Queuing at the peage in Italy to head towards the Mont Blanc tunnel.

Heading back from Italy for the UK, these awkward loads were destined for Whitehaven.

Not what you want to meet on a narrow road with two abnormal loads!

Stunning scenery as the duo make their way from Italy to France.

to him, and he was told that they were going to take veins from his arms instead of the more usual leg. Bob simply said to the surgeon, "You know better than me. If I was fixing your car I would do what I think is best, and so you do what you think is best when fixing my body!"

During his time in hospital he contracted the infection MRSA, and was then moved to his own home for fear of him getting any more infections in the hospital.

> *I was wiped out. One of my wounds just would not heal.*

"I was wiped out. One of my wounds just would not heal. It took months and months, with a local nurse caring for me. But I was determined not to let it beat me. Come the October, I was back on my feet and ready to go back to work again. I approached an agency in Ipswich, filled the various forms out and I was soon told to be at Claydon at 6am Monday morning to meet someone who would give me some work. It was on contract for Argos doing home deliveries."

To this day Bob is still working on contract for Argos. Now it's only two days a week as a truck checker, ensuring the vehicles are not damaged when sent out or on their return, and that their deliveries have all been done. He enjoys working still, even if he is not up the road somewhere.

Residing back in the very house that he was born in, the rest of his spare time is taken up largely by his black Labrador, Harley, and the once stray cat, Moz. As he sits back on his sofa, with the pets vying for the prize space on his lap, he lights up his pipe. I have to ask him, "Do you have any regrets"?

"With hindsight of course I wish we had a better insurance company, but at the time, until they did the dirty on us they had been great. So, if anything, I regret Trans UK folding of course, and wonder what it might have become. If I could have my time again, there would not be much that I would change. My brothers went on to run the family company, and when they sold it, and even when it was running, they were very successful and made a lot of money. But for me, it was always about the experiences. They have not taken a car to the Middle East, for example, or gone out on silly recovery missions. I may have grumbled about some of them at the time, but I more or less enjoyed all of them. Getting out into the world, seeing it through a windscreen, meeting all these different people and seeing how they live and even where they live, that is what I have enjoyed in my life."

Personally, for me too, this is what life is about.

END OF
AN ERA

Bob after lunch at the café enjoying a smoke on his trusty pipe.

B OB PASSED AWAY AT HOME ON 10TH JANUARY 2019, almost a year to
the day since he had finally fully retired. He had been battling cancer and
also a strong chest infection, but he was surrounded by his children, Janie
Jim and Chas, and most close friends had visited him in the last few days. Bright
as a button to the end, I saw him in the afternoon on the 10th, even showing him
a photograph I had picked up recently from another friend, and he remembered
the truck, the driver's name and so on. Michael Coombes and Lenny Balaam have
also sadly passed away since the book was first written.

Bob and former drivers after lunch at the café. L to R: Bob Carter, Paul Doodson, Simon Waspe, Paul Rowlands, Ray Rainham, Eddy English, John Overton, Gerry Keating, Terry 'Smudger' Smith, Brian Wales, Maurice Horrex, Mick Lillie.

I first met Bob after an off the cuff comment to a friend that I knew someone who had driven to the Middle East. That comment led to me doing a bit of research, which led me to Bob. I remember the first time I ever called him on the phone, and the enthusiasm he had straight away. So we arranged a day, and I headed over with my trusty dictaphone to go and 'have a chat'. Well that was around 2004, and those chats never ended, nor did the new information that he remembered constantly.

For the last few years, all of the former drivers along with Bob would meet up every Wednesday lunchtime for lunch at a local transport café. It all started with Bob, Mick Coombes and a couple of others if they were free. It has evolved to more than a dozen former employees, friends, former drivers or colleagues. Former drivers such as Eddie English and Paul Doodson regularly come along, people who I had had no contact with previously when researching the book. What has always left an impression on me is that how everyone has kind words for him; I cannot think of any other boss in transport who could meet up every week with their old employees for lunch. Bob once said to me that had I been older, he certainly would have given me a job at Trans UK, which really touched me.

We took Bob on his final journey on Wednesday, 6th February 2019. I borrowed a 1958 Thames Trader from my old boss, James Harvey at Tannington Transport, similar to what Bob had driven in his early days at the family company. I accompanied the hearse, and even led the cortège in the final metres at the crematorium. Inside it was standing room only, with well-known names in transport attending to pay their final respects. The wake was a happy affair, with everyone sharing some great stories about the man.

Even when helping to arrange the funeral and wake, myself and Bob's children were amazed that the manager of the hotel had a brother who drove for Bob. This is Kim Gladwell, who was Trans UK's youngest driver. In fact, his father agreed to pay the excess on the insurance and so Bob gave him a job.

Bob will truly be missed by many far and wide, but his knowledge and outlook on life and work will live on through many of us. I know the boys will continue to meet every Wednesday, and his legacy will live on through all of them as well as the younger generation, whose influence is far and wide.